D1474005

Homosexuality: A Conversion
*How a Conservative Pastor Outgrew The
Idea That Homosexuality Is A Sin*

The Reverend John H. Tyson, Ph.D.

with

Research Biologist Gregory A. Prince, Ph.D.

Published by eBookIt.com
http://www.eBookIt.com

ISBN-13: 978-1-4566-3227-4 (paperback)
ISBN-13: 978-1-4566-3226-7 (Amazon KDP)
ISBN-13: 978-1-4566-3238-0 (hardcover)

Pictured on cover: temple of Apollo, Corinth

Go Team Fuqua!
You Live Inclusion

Contents

Foreword

Wandering through the ancient city of Ephesus, Turkey, the official tour was finally over. We had seen the usual Roman ruins, broken marble avenues littered with fragments of ancient columns, and the famous facade of the Library of Celsus rising majestically like a post card photograph above the street. Japanese tourists jostled with American, German and Chinese visitors as each group struggled to hear their tour guide, elbow their way to the best position, and take their pictures. I was glad when it was over.

Wending my way from the crowds, I sauntered down a dirt path to find a little solitude on this brutally hot May morning. The wide, bucolic path was somewhat overgrown with bushes and brambles, and I could hear birds twittering and calling. I saw an historic marker pointing the way to "The Church of Mary." Noting that no one else seemed headed in that direction, I followed the sign to the silent ruins.

It had been an enormous basilica. The tremendous girth of the long-broken brick abutments suggested the height and expanse of the soaring arches and vaults they had supported. These formed an irregular cadence on both sides leading to the altar, showing clearly the outlines of the edifice. Ancient marble seats hugged the curve of the apse, and I sat in the center to rest and ponder.

I am seldom spiritually aware of "holy space." It was a ruin, like so many other ruined, vacant churches I had visited on this tour, but it was alive in some way with a sacred presence I cannot describe. It felt like an anteroom of heaven. I sat in silence, soaking in the significance of the spiritually alive and lovely place. This is Mary's church, built in Ephesus, the place where she saw the Church rise mysteriously, gloriously, and irrepressibly; the Church her son gave his life for, the Church she suffered for as no other. This is Mary's church, where in 431 A.D. the Third Ecumenical Council met with bishops and representatives from all Christendom to argue, brawl and maneuver in the debate concerning the title of the Virgin Mary. The unholy, sacred fray which occurred in the basilica was neither the first nor the last in the Church's history; it is just the way the Church does business. Here, Mary was declared not merely *Christotokos* (bearer of Christ) but *Theotokos* (bearer of God). In a unique way, this place is hers.

As I sat envisioning the shouting, the behind-the-scenes deal making, and the open if invisible attendance of heaven, I was overcome with a message I cannot fully describe. The Blessed Mother spoke to me saying, "I am weeping for my homosexual children who are so mistreated by the Church. You must help."

This was unexpected in every possible way.

This experience is so deeply personal, I hesitate to share it. Would the Blessed Mother speak to a Protestant? Would she use the modern word, "homosexual"? What does it mean for the Blessed

Mother to weep? Does this put me on a par with those who see divine images of the Blessed Mother in the shadows of their breakfast muffins? I believe the academic and theological merits of this book can stand on their own, without needing a sprinkle of hocus pocus to recommend it. For all these reasons, I had expected to keep this motivation for writing private. And yet, I want every LGBTQI person to know of God's tender and seeking care for you: that the Lord Jesus sees you, the Lord Jesus loves you, and the Blessed Mother weeps for the pain caused by the Church. She gathers you. She is the Mother of the Church and the Mother of us all. You are precious in the sight of the Lord.

Introduction

Why You Should Read This Book

Until the 1970s, most people agreed that homosexuality was morally wrong. That has now changed. If you have experienced a change of mind and heart, you may find your own story mirrored here. You may also find your personal rationale articulated clearly in terms of the Bible and Christian faith so that you understand your own story better. That is, sometimes you intuitively know what is right without being able to fully explain why. This book will help you find words to explain the "why."

...you will find this book alternately fun, thought-provoking and perhaps, life changing.

If you believe homosexuality is wrong, read this book so you can learn what the other side is thinking. By dealing with these ideas, you may strengthen and refine your own, previously held opinions, and be able to express them better to others. On the other hand, it may cause you to view some things differently.

Either way, you will find this book alternately fun, thought-provoking and perhaps, life changing. No matter which side of this question you are on, you will find your ideas treated with respect and fairness, because almost everyone who is currently on the progressive side of this issue used to be on the conservative side. We have no stones to throw.

This book traces a growing understanding of the interplay between God's love, scripture, the Church, and homosexuality. The renowned medical researcher, Dr. Gregory Prince, wrote the scientific portion of Chapter 5, "Born that Way." There, you will find the latest information about genetics and sexual orientation and identity. The new scientific information on this topic is important, and is placed within a theological context.

Since this is a book of "practical theology," we will apply Christian teachings in a practical way, so you won't need a degree in theology to follow the ideas laid out here. It isn't meant to be the only answer for everyone, but it can help those who struggle to see God's love lived out in Christian community. It may upset you at times, but spiritual growth is often upsetting as it requires us to shed comfortable, inadequate assumptions. On the other hand, this book may feel like an easy and uplifting blessing for you, helping you make sense of some ideas you've held for a long time, but couldn't quite express.

About the Authors

Dr. John Tyson

I am a United Methodist pastor from North Carolina, with the B.A. in Religion and Philosophy from Barton College, two master's degrees from Duke (M.Div. and M.B.A.) and the Ph.D. from the University of Edinburgh, Scotland, in Practical Theology. My doctoral dissertation was focused on John Wesley's doctrine of salvation. I have been a United Methodist pastor for more than thirty years, and for fifteen of those years I taught Biblical studies courses as adjunct faculty at Methodist University in Fayetteville, NC. My books on Conversion and on Church Administration are published by Abingdon.

Because I am a United Methodist pastor and a Wesley scholar, my approach to this question is typically Wesleyan. By "typically Wesleyan" I mean: 1) We believe salvation is available to everyone. 2) We interpret God's will by examining it in the light of scripture, tradition, reason, and experience with an emphasis on scripture. This is often called the "Wesleyan Quadrilateral." 3) We believe that both personal and social holiness are important, so we need to be lovingly careful of how our religious teachings and actions impact both individuals and society. The views shared here are not the official views of any religious organization or church. The journey shared, and the conclusions, are my own. Married to The Reverend Dr. Elizabeth Dodge Tyson, we have five wonderful children, two terrific children-in-law, and two gregarious grandchildren.

Dr. Gregory Prince

I earned the Ph.D. in pathology from UCLA. I spent fifteen years at the National Institutes of Health in Bethesda, Maryland, and then co-founded a biotechnology company focused on respiratory syncytial virus (RSV), the primary cause of infant pneumonia throughout the world. Now in my fifth decade of medical research, I am working to develop new classes of antibiotics against the resistant "superbugs" that have become a major threat to world health. A man of faith, I am privileged to serve on the Board of Governors of Wesley Theological Seminary in Washington, DC. I am married to JaLynn Rasmussen Prince. We have three choice children, the youngest being on the autism spectrum and the focus of our lives.

1

Down Home Religion: Homosexuality Is a Lie from the Pit

Just Confused

I was sitting in Dr. Purcell's religion class at Barton College. He paused in his lecture to ask, "John, what is the conservative eastern North Carolina view on this topic?" Taken by surprise, I replied, "I'm not sure, sir. I haven't researched that."

He responded with humor, "That's alright. Just tell us your opinion."

My religious opinions were pretty much in step with those of conservative people in my region. And why not? Religion was as much a part of my childhood household as fried chicken and banana pudding on Sundays (the recipe is still on the vanilla wafers box- check it out). Jack and Irene Tyson were my paternal grandparents. He was a Free Will Baptist Preacher turned Methodist because he got an education. He and my grandmother had six sons, and they all became Methodist preachers. They were well educated, knew the Lord in a personal way, and preached about God's love and saving power.

Our views on homosexuality were conservative and evangelical mixed with extra grace "when necessary." We believed that God loved everybody, and that at the very least, everybody who loved God back was "saved." I still believe that. Homosexuals were viewed as being "confused." That is, we believed that deep down, everyone was really heterosexual, but some people were confused and didn't realize it. From time to time I heard people say that homosexuality was a "lie from the pit." It was viewed as particularly tragic that these folks were really heterosexuals, but the devil had somehow tricked them into believing otherwise, resulting in much heartache.

> *We believed that God loved everybody, and everybody who loved God back was "saved."*

For people who were heterosexual, the solution seemed pretty simple. "All" someone had to do was to accept the truth that God made them heterosexual, repent of their homosexuality, and accept God's healing and forgiveness. It went without saying that if someone occasionally slipped up but then repented (preferably in private) they would be forgiven, back on the "straight and narrow path." Sunshine and rainbows, but not the gay kind. Getting married was considered a good way to get all kinds of sexual urges regulated. What could go wrong with that?

For those who were not eager to accept the good news that even though they thought they were gay they were actually straight, there was the additional incentive of avoiding hell. Everyone knew there were a few scriptures that supported the notion that homosexuality was immoral, and that sexually immoral people could not enter the kingdom of God. It turns out that these six passages were either misapplied or questionably translated. But since most people just assumed homosexuality was morally wrong anyway, the scriptural basis for this cultural assumption was not examined closely. Therefore we had both positive and negative reinforcement to help people find their "true" sexual identity. The positive reinforcement was the promise of salvation, God's love, and a "normal" life. The negative reinforcement was the threat of hell. The hope was that people would embrace "righteousness" (being straight) out of either love or fear or both. At the time, we thought this approach was progressive, generous, and true.

We Knew that Salvation Was Mysterious

Now we all knew there were exceptions to this logic, and that gay people were certainly not going to hell just because they were gay. We knew that God's grace is immense, God's love is boundless, and everyone lives with some degree of sin in their lives. So if someone "insisted on being homosexual," that was between that person and God. If the person otherwise loved God and neighbor and did not exactly flaunt his or her sex life in the face of the community, then the gay person (who may very well have been a pillar of the church) was certainly saved by God's grace and accepted by the community. It was not at all unusual for old spinster ladies to have lived together all their adult lives out of economy and practicality, since they weren't married anyway. Nor was it very unusual for "confirmed bachelors" to live together for the same reasons. Everyone knew that it was remotely possible that some of these folks might be homosexuals, but no one really knew and no one wanted to know. Often, these folks were leaders in the community, highly valued and dearly loved, if a little "eccentric." Their sexuality was not talked about, so God was free to love them and to forgive them in private, just as he loved and forgave the rest of us for the sins we did not discuss publicly. It was a theological version of "Don't ask, don't tell." The community could believe these nice people were straight, and God could forgive them if they weren't. God's grace and salvation were beautifully mysterious for everyone, including homosexual persons.

It seems surprising today, but sexuality simply was not talked about in church circles as far as I was aware. I heard literally thousands of sermons growing up, and was in Sunday School, prayer meetings and youth groups several times each week. I don't recall ever hearing homosexuality mentioned. There were two reasons for this, I suspect. The first is that specific sins were seldom called out; that would be lewd and vulgar. I don't recall hearing from the pulpit about adultery, fornication, or any other kind of sexual sin because sex simply was not discussed in public, heterosexual or otherwise. But I suspect the other reason homosexuality was not discussed is that most everyone thought it was better to let it sort itself out. Even though there are a few scriptures that may or may not be interpreted to condemn or condone loving and committed homosexual relationships, I never heard these read or referred to from the pulpit. I certainly do not mean to suggest that this silence was universal. This was simply my experience.

This was also my experience in college and in seminary. I was a Religion and Philosophy major in college, but I do not recall homosexuality even having been mentioned. At Duke Divinity School, there was a Gay/Straight Alliance on campus, and I saw its name on one of the office doors, but I never heard anything about it. I do not recall homosexuality being discussed in any of my biblical studies, ministry, or theology classes. However, it was a main topic in my ethics class and senior seminar, where ethics professors labored relentlessly to convince us that homosexuality was morally neutral, like being born left-handed instead of right-handed. We were required to write papers on the subject, and papers which were illiberal were not well received, as I recall.

One particularly crisp memory is from my senior seminar, which was a required class taught by an ethics professor. He began the course by asking, "How many of you are against gay marriage?" I was the only person to raise my hand. Everyone else was wiser, in one way or another, than yours truly. The professor was pleased that he had the vast majority of the class on his side, and he set deftly about his work of marginalizing me:
"And why would you object to gay marriage?"
"Because it is contrary to scripture."

"You, Jerry Falwell, and the other religious right fanatics share the same views on this subject, and anyone who would like to be counted in the same camp as Jerry Falwell is welcome to join you there."

> *This professor treated me like a moron and a bigot...*

This professor treated me like a moron and a bigot, too stupid to deserve either a hearing or an alternative explanation of the scripture. I remember thinking at the time that he was very clever to simply eliminate my objection by grouping me with the one person whom everyone at Duke Divinity School agreed was beyond contempt. I had to give him credit for efficiency. I thought it would have been more honest for us to study the scriptures and unravel any misinterpretation than to simply push that aside as a marginal issue; but he was an ethics professor, not a biblical studies scholar, and Consequentialism (the morality of an action is judged by its consequences) was an acceptable form of ethical reasoning to him. Moreover, the other disciplines such as theology and biblical studies had not yet begun to examine the question of homosexuality in the mainstream. Sometimes the Church changes her understanding of scripture because her understanding of ethics changes first, and we will examine this idea more closely in succeeding chapters.

Cultural and Religious Change

The ethics curriculum at Duke Divinity School was an early signal of cultural and religious change. Even though the Church as I knew it had little to say about homosexuality, and had a quiet attitude of grace on the subject, this does not mean that all of society agreed on a benevolent conspiracy of silence. In 1950, Senator Joseph McCarthy put a public target on the backs of homosexuals in government, saying that they posed a potential blackmail risk. This started a kind of witch hunt for homosexuals working in government which rippled as an undercurrent through mid-century American society with a brief rise in sodomy laws. There were public instances of what we now call hate speech in places of civil discourse, in legislative houses, and on college campuses. Sodomy laws which had been dropped in some states were revived, so that by 1962, the laws were on the books in every state. After this date, sodomy began to be decriminalized, the laws gradually were dropped, and the powerful reaction against the gay witch hunt began.

Interestingly, sodomy laws from colonial times had in their purview all forms of non-procreative sex between married as well as unmarried persons. They had scarcely been enforced because most of the married population was culpable. Their target had not been homosexual persons, a designation which only came about in the late 19th century. The laws were intended to legislate against non-procreative intercourse of any kind, and to protect women, children, and weaker men from abuse, as well as to criminalize bestiality. (See the article by Margot Canaday in the September 22, 2008 issue of <u>The Nation</u> entitled "We Colonials: Sodomy Laws in America.")

Sodomy laws were a kind of legal hyperbole "more honor'd in the breach." Transplanted from ancient English law, sodomy laws were intended partly to satisfy the Church's lingering medieval views that non-procreative sex was sinful. This was the philosophical underpinning for the laws. More practically, they were intended to protect people in exceptional cases from sexual predators and scandalous public display, so they seldom needed to be enforced. This was the case from the beginning for these laws, and one of the reasons they were largely unenforced is that strict enforcement would have made most of the adult population culpable. A recent and famous example is the 1986 Supreme Court case, Hardwick v. Bowers. Hardwick, cited for sodomy, pursued the court action in a bid to have Georgia's sodomy laws declared unconstitutional. District Attorney Lewis Slaton had chosen not to prosecute the sodomy charge, because the occurrence was consensual and occurred in the accused man's own apartment. In this case, the sodomy laws were upheld by the Supreme Court; they were later struck down by the same court in 2003.

Nevertheless, until the 1980s, the Church could live in the comfortable moral ambiguity of "Don't ask, don't tell." This was the unofficial way the church people I knew dealt with the question, and it even became the law for the U.S. military in 1994. During these years, dealing with homosexuality in the parish still tended to be a private matter of counseling between pastor and parishioner, in which the parishioner would be encouraged to accept the truth of his or her heterosexuality, and to accept the forgiveness and healing that Jesus brings. If the healing didn't "work," it was quietly allowed to drop if that was what the parishioner wished. This is the way I learned to deal with these matters as a young pastor, and it remained that way until the AIDS epidemic forced the matter into the public forum. At the first several funerals I did for AIDS victims the deceased were said to have died at a young age from cancer.

The AIDS epidemic catapulted the discussion of homosexuality into the mainstream. Prior to the AIDS epidemic, sexually transmitted diseases in mid-America were treated fairly easily and quietly with antibiotics. Suddenly in the 1980s, gay men and other at risk populations were dying by the tens of thousands from a mysterious and untreatable disease. Although AIDS came to the U.S. in the 1960s, it came to public notice only in the early 1980s. By 1989, the number of reported AIDS cases in the U.S. reached 100,000. People feared contamination from toilet seats or kissing, and homosexuality became a topic which was discussed everywhere, including adult Sunday school classes, but still not from the pulpit as far as I was aware. Ironically, I recall several people in Sunday school classes castigating gay people, without realizing that their own grown sons or daughters were gay. Attitudes towards sex were changing, and gay people were no longer content to pretend to be "eccentric bachelors" or "old maids." With much greater force and consistency, gay people began to insist on equality with straight people. Homosexuality became a hotly debated topic everywhere, including church. People began agitating for gay marriage and the ordination of homosexuals. The days envisioned by my ethics professors had come.

Suddenly, the Church had to do what it didn't want to do. It had to wrestle to the ground the question: Is homosexuality a sin? We are still wrestling. For a variety of reasons which we will look at honestly, this is very difficult to resolve. The traditional approach, as already described, was to assume that if people loved the Lord and behaved themselves decently in society, they would be "saved." Exactly how God would do this was up to God, but God's love and grace are so profound that God is able to save all sinners, "even me" as the scriptures and the hymn writers say. Denominations with Calvinist theological underpinnings could rely on God's sovereignty to elect mysteriously to salvation any whom he called- gay, straight, or otherwise, and denominations with Armenian leanings could rely on God's saving grace for all repentant sinners.

However, this quiet and inadequate approach would no longer suffice because questions about marriage, church membership, and ordination had to be answered: for example, is it okay to have homosexual pastors? Rather quickly, the old social consensus about homosexuality disappeared. Until the 1970s, homosexuality had been regarded by the Church as a sin, by the government as a crime, and by the medical community as a mental disorder. That was changing with surprising speed. In 1973 homosexuality was removed from the

American Psychiatric Association's manual of mental disorders and replaced by the category, "Sexual Orientation Disturbance." Today, the standard of psychotherapy in the U.S. and Europe is gay affirmative psychotherapy, which encourages gay people to accept their sexual orientation. In 2003, the supreme court ruled that sodomy laws were unconstitutional, and in 2015 gay marriage was legalized in all fifty states. The Church is still struggling to clarify its thinking and practice, and several denominations have split over this question. Some denominations embrace the pre-1970s ideas I've outlined above, while others have come to believe that the mistreatment of homosexual people, rather than homosexuality, is the moral issue. Still other denominations waver between the two, unsure.

What About Scripture?

It is self-defeating for progressive Christians to take moral stands without understanding how those positions are informed by scripture. And yet it is equally self-defeating for conservative Christians to take stands that are not required by scripture, which even non-Christians recognize as morally wrong. I was recently at a large denominational meeting to discuss LGBTQI issues. A conservative voice from the audience said, "We believe the Bible." A progressive voice then responded: "So do we." Students of church history would have experienced *deja vu*. The Church has been here before, many times, with people on both sides of a moral issue claiming scriptural support.

A conservative voice said, "We believe the Bible." A progressive voice responded: "So do we."

Before we begin to look at individual scriptures, I'd like to spend a little time thinking about how the Bible was formed, and the tools we use to interpret difficult, obscure, or contradictory passages. We'll do that in the next chapter, and then we will begin to apply those tools in the chapters that follow.

Questions for Reflection and Discussion

1. What were your views on homosexuality when you were growing up?

2. Have your views changed over the years?

3. How does God's grace work to bring us to salvation when we carry deep-seated sin?

4. Does everyone carry deep-seated sin, perhaps without realizing it?

5. How did Gay Liberation change society's views on homosexuality?

For Further Research: Do an internet search of sodomy laws.

2

A Few Principles of Biblical Interpretation

Before going to seminary, I had never thought much about how to interpret the Bible. I just loved it, read it, and applied what I could. Whenever I read something I didn't understand, I would mentally set it aside until I had "more light." Sometimes I would read things in the Bible that I understood quite clearly, but they just did not seem applicable to today; for example, some of the Old Testament ceremonies. As I attended seminary, finished the Ph.D., and later taught Old and New Testament at Methodist University, I learned a lot more about how to interpret the Bible. These tools for biblical interpretation, which took about twenty-five years to master, gave me a solid foundation for interpreting the Bible in more difficult areas such as the role of women in Church and society. During these years, I was a firm traditionalist concerning the question of homosexuality.

Before we can truly understand the Bible on controversial subjects, we have to get a few principles of biblical interpretation under our belts. I realize that "principles of biblical interpretation" may not sound fascinating, but stick with me, because I think you'll like it. If we can understand how our view of scripture informs our faith, our faith will be much stronger. It will also help us create a framework to interpret difficult scriptures like the ones dealing with homosexuality. We will deal with the idea of scripture as the word of God, and what it means to take the Bible literally. We will also be alerted to literary devices and culturally conditioned assumptions.

I Literally Jumped Over the Moon

Intuitively, we understand that the writers of the Bible use language in all the varieties and genres we do. Some is written as history, some as poetry set to music, some as law, some as biography, some as wisdom, some as drama, some as advice, some as solutions to a laundry list of questions, and some as wild, apocalyptic code. We don't read a biography the same way we read a science textbook, and we don't read legal documents the same way we read poetry. Different genres or categories of writing are read with different expectations, and each genre can convey truth in its own way. The writers of scripture use metaphor, allegory, allusion, idiom, hyperbole and every other literary device. So when someone says they take the entire Bible literally, this can be mystifying.

There is a great deal of disagreement, argument, and even ill will among Christians about taking the Bible literally. Some say they take the entire Bible literally, and they tend to distrust those who do not. Others say they understand the Bible figuratively and are appalled at those who say they take the entire Bible literally. I'm going to let you in on a secret paradox: those who cherish the Bible as containing God's word take the whole thing literally, and yet no one who cherishes the Bible as containing God's word takes the whole thing literally. These two statements seem mutually exclusive, and yet they are both true. The reason for this is that the word "literally" has two opposite meanings. The first, formal, and primary meaning of "literally" is to take words in their usual or most basic sense without metaphor or allegory. And yet the secondary, informal meaning of the word is exactly the opposite: using words metaphorically or allegorically for emphasis while not being literally true. If you look up the word, "literally," you'll find both these definitions, and Miriam Webster addresses the frustration created by the two opposite uses of the word. The Oxford English Dictionary even chronicles the secondary use of the word, demonstrating a long and impressive pedigree.

No rational person takes the entire Bible literally in the primary sense of the word. Progressives are dumbfounded when they meet someone who says they take the entire Bible literally. They wonder, "how can anyone be so irretrievably stupid?" And conservatives often triumphantly perpetuate this tug of war by pretending that they do indeed take the entire Bible literally, without metaphor or symbol. But of course, they do not. For example, Psalm 18:2 says, "God is my rock and my fortress." No church holds as doctrine the idea that God is a literal, physical rock; that would be animism and idolatry. When Jesus tells us to gouge out our right eye if it causes us to sin (Matthew 5), we all understand that this is hyperbole, which is exaggeration to emphasize a point. Otherwise, there would be a lot of one-eyed conservative Christians. And when Jesus says, in John 15, that he is the vine and we are the branches, no one believes that Jesus is reduced to a literal grapevine with leaves coming out his ears and grape bunches hanging off his arms, or that his followers are literal grape vine branches. Everyone naturally understands that Jesus is using a metaphor, bringing us to the second definition of "literally," which is actually, "figuratively."

This is the tricky part. Progressives, who say they do not take the entire Bible literally, are relying on the first and primary meaning of the word. Conservatives, who say they do take the entire Bible literally, are relying on both meanings of the word, which seems like cheating. Why would they do that? Perhaps because conservatives prize the fact that they take the Bible literally whenever possible, and in order to emphasize this point they cheat a little and say they take the whole thing literally. This may be an exaggeration, but they feel it is more true than not. And they may feel that admitting that they don't take the entire Bible literally puts them on a slippery slope theologically. So by "entire Bible" they mean "most of the Bible" and by "literally" they mean "sometimes literally, but always seriously." There is good biblical tradition for this. Sometimes in Greek, "pas," translated "all" doesn't literally mean "all" but it means, "all the ones in this group." In this case, it would mean, "I take all the Bible literally that I take literally." Of course, a simple test for a sincere reader who thinks they take the entire Bible literally, in its first definition, is to read the Bible, and as they read to ask themselves: "Do I think this section is meant literally, or not?" Pretty soon, they will have their answer.

All this is complicated as the second definition of "literally" comes into play. These are probably the people who will say something like, "I was so angry I literally exploded" or "I was so happy I was literally over the moon." But of course, they did not literally explode, nor did they literally jump over the moon. They are just using "hyperbole." The dictionary says that hyperbole is an extreme form of exaggeration, not meant to be taken literally, in order to make a point forcefully. And yet, the two opposite dictionary definitions of "literally" cloud this issue a bit because the two definitions embrace both ideas. So people do not take the entire Bible literally in the sense that they take the most basic meaning of scripture's words without metaphor, symbolism or allegory. But they may take the entire Bible literally in the sense that they accept the plain, literal meaning of the words unless a metaphorical meaning is called for. This brings us neatly to a consideration of John Wesley's views on the subject.

How Wesley Interpreted Scripture

Many Protestant denominations (both conservative and progressive) use the eighteenth century Church leader and founder of Methodism, John Wesley, as a source of sound theological teaching. Wesley teaches that scripture should be taken in its plain, literal meaning unless: it is contrary to reason, experience, ethical behavior, other more basic scriptures, God's nature of justice, mercy and love, or unless it is culture bound. (For an excellent article on this, see John Wesley's Non-Literal Literalism and Hermeneutics of Love by Rem B. Edwards. Wesleyan Theological Journal 1986: 51, 2, 26-40).

For example, Wesley famously disagrees with his fellow methodists such as George Whitefield, James Hervey, and Augustus Toplady on the subject of unconditional predestination. You may recall that these disagreements are called the "Calvinistic Controversies" and can be found in most any Wesley biography. Although these men are able to point to a small handful of scriptures that seem to teach unconditional predestination, Wesley interprets these scriptures otherwise because he believes that unconditional predestination contradicts the "whole tenor of scripture." A major theme of scripture is that Christ comes so that "*whosoever* believeth in him should not perish but have everlasting life." Wesley believes that the Calvinistic conclusions of double predestination- the idea that people are absolutely predestined by God either to heaven or to hell and the person can do nothing to change that- turn the entirety of scripture on its ear, making God more evil than the devil. (See John Wesley's sermon, "Free Grace" especially sections 2 and 4.) Therefore, Wesley interprets scriptures which reference predestination as operating within an overarching interpretation, or hermeneutic, of human freedom to respond to the love and grace of God in Christ. A few of the scriptures that seem to support absolute predestination are found in Paul's writings, but some of the scriptures that seem to support the opposite view (genuine freedom to respond to God's grace) are also found in Paul's writings. Those who subscribe to the doctrine of unconditional predestination quote Paul. Those who subscribe to "free grace" also quote Paul. Certainly Paul does not believe he contradicts himself, so the answer lies in the realization that scripture must be used to interpret scripture, and that overarching themes of scripture must be used to interpret more obscure passages. Of course, some people simply like the doctrine of unconditional predestination and so on this point, they choose to interpret scripture in the way that suits them best. We will come back to Wesley's method of interpreting scripture in future chapters, as we look at the six scriptures that are said to refer to homosexuality. For now, the point is that there is scriptural support for opposing views in most ethical and theological questions. The question revolves around how we interpret scripture.

Conservative or Progressive?
Are you more conservative or more progressive? The answer revolves around how heavily you weigh scripture and tradition in making your

decisions about right and wrong. Conservatives and progressives give different answers and incur different risks.

By the way, please forgive the broadness of language concerning "conservative" and "progressive" Christians. You and I both know that these are relative generalizations with inexact meanings. Someone can be progressive on some issues and conservative on others. And yet, this characterization is useful for our conversation, because even though it is a very broad generalization, it is a place holder for identifying differing views. In general, I use the term "conservative" to identify a tendency to rely more heavily on traditional understandings of scripture as we consider change. Similarly, I use the term "progressive" for those who embrace what they see as positive change, even if the connections with scripture and tradition are unclear. Others may use these terms in different ways. I have genuine respect for both conservative and progressive views when motivated by love for God and neighbor. But either way, it is not helpful for conservatives to make important judgments based on a superficial understanding of scripture, nor is it helpful for progressives to make important judgments by simply ignoring the Bible. An important leader in my church gave me an unexpected lesson on this.

You Actually Believe that Stuff?

Progressive Christians sometimes find it horrifying when I say that I believe the Bible. This mystifies me. How do people lead a Christian life if they do not believe the Bible? Indeed, why do they bother to try? If the Bible is simply a collection of outdated stories and myths to be left unread on the shelf, then how do these folks piece together their faith? I do not know, and I'm not sure they know, either. And yet many of these Christians have a strong and beautiful faith without ever looking closely at their system for interpreting scripture. This is testimony to the power of the Church to shape faith positively and beautifully through worship, preaching, testimony, service and fellowship, even when people are allergic to the authority of scripture.

For example, years ago, an important leader in my congregation said, "We don't like it when you preach from the Old Testament. We don't really believe any of that, and would appreciate it if you would stop referring to it." I listened until he finished what he had to say, and thanked him for sharing his viewpoint with me. I had no intention of arguing with him, or of committing heresy by omitting the Old Testament from my future preaching, but I did listen and thank him for his candor. To be fair, his view is not unheard of.

Many people view the Old Testament as more difficult, more confounding, and less relevant than the New. And you may recall that as early as 147 A.D., a theologian named Marcion eliminated the Old Testament from his official list of scriptures. You may also recall he was officially branded a heretic.

Several months later, this same church leader came to me again saying, "we don't like it when you preach from Paul. We don't agree with his theology, and we really don't like him personally." Again, I listened attentively, and thanked him for sharing his viewpoint. I was not exactly shocked. There are many Christians who do not appreciate Paul, probably because our modern day is culturally so different from Paul's world. However, many scholars attribute up to 30% of the New Testament to Paul's authorship. So dumping Paul's writings from one's personal list of sacred texts thins it considerably; but for people who seldom read the Bible anyway, this may not seem like much of a loss.

Again, several months later, the church leader came to me. I had preached from Luke's gospel that day about the Rich Man and Lazarus (Luke 16:19-31), and the importance of helping the poor. The church leader said, "I don't know where you got all this heaven and hell stuff you were preaching about today, but you need to know that this congregation doesn't believe in that stuff, and we don't like it when you talk about it." I responded half-playfully and half-seriously: "About a year ago you told me this congregation does not like the Old Testament. And about six months ago, you told me this congregation does not like any of the Pauline texts. As to where I got today's text, it was from Jesus in Luke's gospel. So you're telling me this congregation doesn't like the Old Testament, the Epistles, or the Gospels. I am making an educated guess that you do not speak for the entire congregation but primarily for yourself. Since you reject the entire canon of scripture, have you considered embracing a different religion?"

To be fair, this leader had a strong and beautiful faith in many ways, but he had no discernible respect for scripture. This extreme example helped me to understand forcefully that many Christians do not view the scripture in the same way I do. They view it as a collection of quaint stories rendered opaque, and largely irrelevant, by distant time and culture. They do not view scripture as containing the word of God; they view scripture as an entirely human construct. These folks believe what they please and don't bother themselves much about what scripture says. They do not submit themselves to the authority of scripture, or wrestle to forge a unity of scripture, tradition, reason, and experience as they shape their faith; instead, they rely mostly on reason, experience, and whichever way their wind is blowing. Sometimes that is useful to the Church. Remember Galileo?

The Human and Divine In Scripture

I view scripture as containing the word of God. I treasure and revere every word of it. However, that does not mean that a divine finger wrote the Bible and then dropped it out of the sky, nor does it mean that God dictated the scriptures letter by letter and word by word to the writer. Some religions specifically do believe these things about their scriptures. Christianity is not one of them.

So how were the scriptures formed? In a nutshell, people experienced God, and then wrote about it under the inspiration of the Holy Spirit, for and within the faith community. Christian scripture was birthed by God through the faith community, and like Jesus himself, it is both divine and human. We see its

. .. that does not mean that a divine finger wrote the Bible and then dropped it out of the sky.

divinity as it reveals the grace, love, and power of God in Christ. We see its humanity in stories and settings which are bound by time and culture, and yet in many ways transcend both. We see its humanity in manuscripts copied meticulously by hand, and sometimes emended with the best of intentions. We see its humanity in texts and theological understandings which gently update or correct previous texts as Matthew appears to do in a few places with Mark's gospel, and as the New Testament provides a dramatic new lens through which to view the Old. We see the Bible's humanity as the writers mention people in their local faith communities, as Luke mentions Salome, and as Paul mentions Priscilla and Aquila. Moreover, all of these writings are approved and canonized by the Church. Other gospels, religious texts, and letters were written which the Church did not ultimately elevate to the status of scripture. The reason this matters is that the Church ultimately decided, by practice, tradition, argument and divine inspiration, what writings would be recognized as rising to the level of authoritative scripture. This was a sifting process that took a few hundred years in the hands of ordinary Christ lovers like those who lead the Church today.

What does this mean for us? It means that scripture should be handled with extreme respect, delicacy and care. It is sacred, containing the message and teachings of God. And yet, the progressive revelation of scripture is genuinely a product of the culture and time where it was written. To treat scripture properly, we should not just ignore it as irrelevant and incomprehensible. And yet, neither can we ignore the fact that God's word comes fully clothed in a time and culture removed from us by thousands of years. This often makes interpretation difficult, and sometimes impossible. For example, the exact meaning of the Hebrew word "selah," used 74 times in the Old Testament, is lost. We can only infer what it means from its context.

The Bible contains the word of God for us, and we feed on it hungrily, lovingly, and reverently. In this way we are guided by God daily, and we grow spiritually strong and mature. And yet, we must not be lazy or undisciplined in our reading of scripture. Before we can understand what God's word says to us today, we must understand what it meant to its original hearers. Before we can apply God's word to our own lives, we must understand both the divine intention of God and the sweep of human context in which it was written. This is often difficult. Some people respond to this difficulty by simply dismissing scripture as too complex to understand: "Preacher, we don't like it when you preach from the Old Testament." Yet, others respond by oversimplifying the problem to a bumper sticker: "God said it, I believe it, that settles it." That axiom may sound reassuring, but these folks would probably shrink from a bumper sticker that read: "Execute Rebellious Children" (Deuteronomy 21:18-21). Both extremes can be shallow. If we are serious about loving the word of God and about discerning divine will, we must be serious and systematic in learning to interpret scripture.

Culture Bound

Wesley mentions the problem of scripture that is "culture bound." We must admit that in some ways the writers of scripture were limited to their cultural world views, while in other ways their vision extended into eternity. A classic image for this problem of biblical interpretation is that the word of God is like a bundle of wheat. Most of the wheat plant is inedible, including the stalk and hull. It is easy enough to cut the grains of wheat from the stalk, but separating the nutritious wheat kernel from its hull is not so easy. It requires a labor-intensive process of beating or threshing the wheat to loosen the hull, and then winnowing to separate the loosened hull from the kernel. Of course, the work is worth the effort. This analogy is often applied to understanding the Bible. The life-giving kernel of God's eternal truth is there, but it is carried by a cultural "husk." We must look carefully to discern the cultural husk and then work to separate it from the kernel of God's eternal truth to discern God's truth for us today. Not everyone agrees on what is husk and what is kernel. While it is true that the nature of God does not change, God reveals God's will and truth to us progressively (John 14:26) as we are changed from one degree of glory to another (II Cor. 3:18).

A few minutes ago, I mentioned Galileo, the Renaissance scientist. Working from Copernicus' views, Galileo taught that the earth revolved around the sun rather than vice-versa. This contradicted the traditional and ancient assumption that the earth was stationary, and that the sun moved, rising and setting. Since the cultural assumption was that the sun moved rather than the earth, this found its way into several scriptures because the scriptures are partly a product of the cultural assumptions of the writers. Since scripture then seemed to support the idea of geocentrism, Galileo's views were deemed contrary to scripture and tradition and therefore heretical. After his trial, he was convincingly threatened with torture and placed under house arrest for the rest of his days.

It has been said that the chilling effect of Galileo's trial marked the end of the Renaissance, as Galileo's world of humanism and science collided with the power of the Catholic Church. Not only did we, the Church, tragically mistreat Galileo and others because of the hubris of our scriptural interpretation, we associated a sickening odor with the body of Christ which has not fully dissipated 500 years later.

Galileo's trial illustrates a tragic circular argument that can occur with scripture and tradition. Since something is "common sense" and traditionally accepted as true, it easily becomes part of the cultural assumptions of the writers of scripture. Since it is written in scripture, it must be true. Since it is scripturally true it must be enforced, even if the enforcement is so inhumane that much of the civilized world shrinks from the Church in unrelenting disgust. I think we have done exactly this with our understanding of homosexuality and LGBTQI people.

My guess is that some gentle reader even now is looking up scriptures about geocentrism and exclaiming that the Bible really does not teach this. That is my point, exactly. Biblical writers assumed a geocentric universe and used that worldview to express theological truths. Both Catholics and Protestants assumed a geocentric worldview until science was accepted which proved otherwise, and they cited verses from the Bible as proof of their assumptions. In the book of Joshua (10:12-13), for example, we read that Joshua asked God to stop the sun from moving so he could finish fighting a battle in daylight. Scripture says, "The sun stopped in the middle of the sky and delayed going down about a full day." This geocentric miracle is repeated in the book of Habakkuk (3:11) where we read that "sun and moon stood still in the heavens..." Because the writers assumed that God held the sun still in order to extend the day, they described it that way. They were recording a miracle within the constraints of their cultural understanding and worldview. Other scriptures indicate the same worldview, such as Psalm 19:4-6 and Ecclesiastes 1:5. Not only does the scripture ascribe movement to the sun, it explicitly states that the earth does not move. For example, Psalms 93:1 and 96:1 read, "the world. . .cannot be moved." These passages, and the others referenced above, were used during Galileo's trial. And although we now understand that these scriptures were misappropriated, the Church certainly did not think so at the time of the trial.

We can now see that the Bible never taught geocentricity as such; rather, this cultural worldview was assumed by the writers as they expressed their theological truths using "phenomenological language." This happens when the writer uses words to describe his or her experience, whether or not it is scientifically accurate. That is, the sun appears to rise and set, and the biblical writers use phenomenological language to describe it. It described what the writer experienced, without necessarily describing what actually happened from a scientific viewpoint.

When the writers of scripture said "the world cannot be moved" they probably did not have in mind questions of geocentricity (earth centered, not moving) versus heliocentricity (sun centered, not moving). Rather, they were expressing theological truths about the constancy and dependability of God's care. And yet, the Church rather naturally drifted into the idea that the scriptures clearly teach that the sun moves and the earth doesn't. The Bible, the Church's tradition, and universal experience all taught that the earth is stationary and the sun moves, and this belief was sufficient to fuel a widely publicized trial that brought a severe sentence upon the man who contradicted it. And yet we now know that our interpretation of scripture, tradition and experience was just wrong. There are at least 73 scriptures stating that the earth cannot move, or that the sun does, and these scripture references are found in the Old Testament, the Gospels and the Epistles. We now know that these scriptures are just phenomenological, some of us would call them figures of speech. We ourselves speak of the sun rising and setting without intending to invoke the notion of geocentricity. But there was a time when the Church did not view it that way at all. The Church viewed these cultural assumptions as revealed truth.

As we read and study the scriptures, we must learn to separate the eternal word of God from culture bound assumptions of the authors. This is often difficult. Therefore, some reject the authority of scripture altogether rather than to do this hard work, while others dig in their heels and refuse to change even when a greater light shows them to be in error. For instance, there is an internet preacher who proclaims that since the Bible teaches that the earth does not move, all preachers should proclaim geocentrism as literal truth. Can you imagine how ridiculous this would make the Church appear? The Church always winds up looking ridiculous, or worse, cruel, when it clings to understandings of scripture that turn out to have been wrong. People have historically been mistreated when the Bible, the Church's tradition, and experience have been mis-interpreted, leading to the wrong conclusions. This is one of the problems we have in interpreting God's will for LGBTQI persons. Are the traditional ways of viewing homosexuality an instance of misinterpreting the Bible?

Importantly, our chief concern is not whether the Church "looks good" to the world. Since sharing the good news of Jesus Christ is fundamental to God's call for the Church, we are always concerned

...many choose to err on the side of generosity, love, and grace.

about how we appear to the world. Are we Christ-like? Are we kind and just? Are we seen to manifest the love and grace of God in Jesus Christ? But even more important than how we appear to the world, is how we appear to Jesus Christ, for we are his body. It is tragic for the Church, the body of Jesus Christ, when we misrepresent him to the world. What if we are misrepresenting homosexuality to the world as a sin, when it is actually a culture bound prejudice against a minority group? On the other hand, what if progressives err when we say homosexuality is not a sin? Perhaps we must err on one side or the other. Many choose to err on the side of generosity, love, and grace.

Questions for Reflection and Discussion

1. Are some parts of scripture more authoritative for you than others? If so, what are they?

2. Would you describe yourself as more conservative, or more progressive in your religious views? Why?

3. Do you take the Bible literally, figuratively, or both? What does that mean to you?

4. John Wesley teaches that scripture should be taken in its plain, literal meaning unless: it is contrary to reason, experience, ethical behavior, other more basic scriptures, or God's nature of justice, mercy and love, or unless it is culture bound. Do you agree?

5. The Bible says the sun moves and the earth doesn't. How do you deal with that?

6. Did Galileo get a fair shake? What motivated the Church to treat him as they did? How might this be like or unlike the Church's current treatment of LGBTQI people?

For Further Research: Read Rem B. Edwards' important article entitled "John Wesley's Nonliteral Literalism and the Hermeneutics of Love" in the Wesleyan Theological Journal: 51, 2, 26-40. Just do an internet search of the title and the article will appear.

3

Conservatives, Progressives, and Jesus

How Change Happens

Much of my work in the Duke MBA program dealt with leadership and the management of change in organizations. One of the reasons this is important is that organizations can become stalled or decline when change is not managed well. When things work normally, there is a rather predictable way that change spreads within an organization. This formula was developed by E. M. Rogers in the 1960s, and various versions of it are widely used to give a broad view of the diffusion of innovation. First, there are the Innovators. These are the people who have a new idea, and they make up about 2.5% of the group. Once these passionate people get organized and begin to spread their idea, about 13.5% of the group agree immediately with the new idea. These are the Early Adopters. They are the kind of people who are always on the lookout for positive change, and they are very proud of this; it is an important part of their self-identity. At this point, about 16% of the group are on the side of change, with 84% against the change. Next come the 34% who are the Early Majority Adopters. These are leaders who understand the idea and have had time to see its value. They have come to believe in the new idea and now put their weight behind it. Suddenly, there is a shift or tipping point in the majority viewpoint. The next group are the Late Majority Adopters. These are the next 34% who shift their view point quite quickly, once they realize that a majority of others have. They are willing to follow whatever the majority thinks. Now 84% of the group are fully behind the new idea. The remaining 16% are called Laggards, and many of them will never, never, never change. They firmly believe they are right, everyone else is wrong, and they will not compromise their principles. They may be the folks who are still flying the Stars and Bars 150 years after Appomattox. Or they may be the folks who think preachers should proclaim a geocentric universe because they alone truly believe this is what the Bible teaches.

Concerning homosexuality, my guess is that we are beyond the 50% tipping point. According to the Pew Research Center for Religion and Public Life, 62% of Americans believe homosexuality should be accepted; 36% of Evangelical Protestants, 66% of Mainline Protestants, and 70% of Catholics agree. 83% of those who are not religiously affiliated agree, with the numbers growing each year (www.pewforum.org/religious-landscape-study/views-about-homosexuality). In other words, those of us who are just now figuring out that homosexuality is not a sin are not heroes or progressives. Instead, we are at best "Late Majority Adopters" who are in danger of becoming weirdos, the religious version of the hard-bitten little Confederate soldier caricature who carries the slogan, "Forgit Hell!" We should be aware that others have seen a light which we have not yet been able to recognize. Even if we cannot yet discern that light from so great a distance, we should listen carefully and seriously to progressives as they describe it.

Conservatives do not want to discover that we have become Pharisees and Sadducees while trying to avoid heresy and apostasy (abandonment of right belief). It tends to be the conservatives who steady the boat and keep it from capsizing in the winds of change; our role is crucial in that regard. But the progressives move the boat forward. Conservatives have to be watchful so that as the boat moves forward, we are not simply left behind, irrelevant. When increasing moral light shows that it is time to let go, we need to move forward gracefully.

In every age, there are conservatives who become a byword, the face of intransigence, bigotry and hatred. Christian conservatives are quickly becoming that face concerning the LGBTQI community. I realize that many of us conservatives don't feel threatened by this image. We are comfortable being in the minority because we are convinced that "right" is on our side. The trouble for conservatives is that in many ways, "right" is not static. It develops. It moves. It shifts under our feet as we try to keep our balance.

Does "Right" Change?

In Chapter Two, we defined what we meant by the categories of conservatives and progressives, and the positive roles both play. Next, I'd like to place the current question in context by looking at several instances of how this tug of war between conservatives and progressives has played out in history. What we will see is a gradual unfolding of how the love and grace of Jesus Christ changes the way we treat the "other." The other, at first seen as "less than" is eventually recognized as fully human, enlarging and enriching the Christian family circle.

There is a famous hymn, "Once to Every Man and Nation," written by James Russell Lowell. As a young man I liked the hymn a great deal. I liked the dramatic triplets that recurred at just the right moments, I liked the majestic march-like rhythm, the moving bass line, and the imposing sense of dramatic destiny. However, one thing about this hymn always annoyed me. There is a line that declares, "time makes ancient good uncouth."

I told you I am a conservative, so the suggestion that virtue evolves over time raised my hackles. When I was younger, I had a strong sense that righteousness, goodness, and virtue are like platonic ideals that never change, and their characteristics are eternal. This is certainly true if the foundation is broad enough: "Love God supremely and your neighbor as yourself." But as Jesus' greatest moral teaching is unpacked and applied, brought down to earth into the hurly-burly of everyday living, and massaged and manipulated to fit the cramped quarters of our moral capacities, there is much room for interpretation, much allowance for shrinkage, and much room for growth.

As I have grown older, I have had to admit that Lowell is right. Somehow, as the morality of Christian society grows through the centuries, ideas and practices that used to seem kind and generous now seem reprehensible and self-serving.

For example, our nation is having such a moment now. Slave-holders who were as highly respected as they were wealthy left large endowments to universities. These grateful universities were only too happy to name buildings to honor their benefactors, forever twining the names of the venerated institutions with the names of the venerable families. But suddenly, these universities are in crisis because their venerable benefactors, with the passage of time, have rather suddenly come to be viewed with nauseating opprobrium. The universities now appear to glorify human oppression on a vast scale. Emergency board meetings are held, statues are removed secretly in the dead of night, and buildings are renamed for those who are today's moral heroes. Lowell is right. Time makes ancient good uncouth. If we would keep up with virtue's march, even conservatives must occasionally run in our wing-tips and pumps to catch up. Yesterday's lies and rationalizations about righteousness are now seen for what they are.

If we would keep up with virtue's march, even conservatives must occasionally run in our wing-tips and pumps to catch up.

For that very practical reason, I would like to frame the question about whether homosexuality is a sin within the larger context of other changes of morality within the Church. There is a healthy and God-glorifying moral growth that takes place within individuals as we grow in grace, and within the Church as we grow more and more into the likeness of Christ. This growth is sometimes painful and ugly, involving moral outrage on both sides. Debates become public brawls, and there is bloodletting which is usually only figurative but is sometimes quite literal. The process is gut-wrenching. But it is a process repeated through history as the Church refines and reforms herself from time to time.

For conservatives, framing the question within this context may seem like sleight of hand, as though I am trying to somehow evade the clear meaning and impact of scripture. That isn't the case. As I have struggled theologically with this issue for the past 30 years, I have slowly come to realize there is a pattern here. The question of whether homosexuality is a sin is not a unique case. I have gradually recognized that it is part of a pattern of other questions the Church has dealt with, such as the first century "Gentile problem," the sixteenth century "Reformation problem," the nineteenth century "slavery problem," the twentieth century "race problem," and the twentieth century "sexism problem." Now we have the twenty-first century "homosexual problem." As I came to understand how the Church dealt with scripture and tradition in these previous problems, I began to see a pattern. People's consciences were quickened by the Holy Spirit, and they began to see the status quo in a new light. That new light revealed something ugly and inadequate, an ethic formed by prejudice and privilege; an ethic not yet fully immersed in the love of God revealed in Jesus through the continuing work of the Holy Spirit.

Once the Holy Spirit gives us eyes to see that ugliness, we can't "unsee" it. We see scripture, and people, in a new light. Somehow with the passage of time, the Holy Spirit broadens and sharpens our vision of right and wrong, like an optician who changes lenses and says, "can you see better now?" The bottom line of letters was always on the eye chart, but it was simply an irrelevant blur until our increased vision enabled us to see with crisp clarity a whole new line of letters. Similarly, the Holy Spirit quickens our minds and hearts to see an injustice which had been blurred before.

Jesus Christ and the Conservative Religious Establishment

For Christians, the ultimate historical struggle between conservatives and progressives is the struggle between Jesus and the Jewish religious leaders of his day. The conservative, intransigent religious establishment loathed and feared Jesus partly because he reinterpreted everything in both scripture and tradition through the lens of himself as the Christ, the unique and pre-existent Son of God. This seemed the outer limit of heresy. I absolutely sympathize with the conservatives, for Jesus was right when he said from the cross, "Father, forgive them; they don't know what they do." They did not know. They thought their hatred was pleasing to God. They thought their rejection of Jesus would keep society rightly ordered. They were definitely on the side of scripture as interpreted by their tradition, but we can see that scripture had been incorrectly appropriated by skewed tradition.

As heirs of the ultimate progressive, Jesus Christ, Christians should look first at how Jesus dealt with both scripture and tradition. It is fair to say that Jesus taught that he was uniquely one with God, and the Church's bedrock doctrine of the Trinity (one God in three persons: Father, Son, and Holy Spirit) confirms that fact. The Trinity is the cornerstone of Christian faith. This also demonstrates that the Jews were correct when they accused Jesus of a teaching which they perceived as a pernicious, blatant blasphemy. That is, the Jews did not misunderstand Jesus' teaching, but they violently disagreed with it. In this teaching, Jesus was seen to defy the traditional Jewish understanding of the *Shemah*, one of the most important theological formulations of Judaism: "Hear O Israel: the Lord our God, the Lord our God is one." This is a clash of the Titans when it comes to progressive/conservative challenges. The conservatives were certain they were on the right side of history. They thought Jesus had to be wrong because in their view he was contradicting both scripture and tradition at the very core. But even though Jesus was dramatically reinterpreting scripture and tradition, Christians believe he was right.

Scriptural Application Changes

There have always been serious and sincere questions about when a certain teaching of scripture has been surpassed by a more profound moral code, and there have always been people who used these questions to generate more heat than light. This was certainly true of Jesus' teachings in Matthew's gospel. Jesus had the audacity to radically change the teachings of Moses, clearly and directly. In Matthew's Sermon on the Mount, Jesus cited the laws of Moses and pulled a James Russell Lowell. . .or did Lowell pull a "Jesus"? Jesus declared, "You have heard that it was said by them of old time...but I declare unto you..." Jesus did this with teachings about murder, adultery, swearing oaths, revenge, and love for enemies (Matthew 5:21-44). In this way, Jesus cited scripture and specifically surpassed it with new teaching.

There are important implications here. One is that Jesus is greater than Moses, which was shocking to Jesus' contemporary religious conservatives. This flew in the face of their understanding of both scripture and tradition. Another is that scripture sometimes needs reinterpretation. Allow me to repeat this idea, because it is a very important one: scripture sometimes needs reinterpretation. As Lowell has it, "time makes ancient good uncouth."

Jesus took various teachings from the Old Testament and changed them to reflect a more perfect moral code. The idea was that these teachings on adultery, revenge, and anger were progressive when they were first laid out in the law of Moses, advancing human understanding of justice and righteousness. But by Jesus' day, more than one thousand years later, some of the Old Testament teachings were no longer progressive. They were not advancing moral righteousness, but limiting it, so Jesus reinterpreted them. For example, when the Old Testament taught "an eye for an eye and a tooth for a tooth" (Exodus 21:24) it was helpfully limiting the scope of revenge. Retaliation was limited to the degree of injury inflicted by the original crime. This was a moral improvement over the unlimited revenge that was sometimes exacted in Old Testament culture. But in Matthew 5:38-48, Jesus reinterpreted this moral teaching. He taught his followers to "turn the other cheek" and "love your enemy."

We can see this updating of the moral code again in the famous story of the woman caught in the act of adultery. Jesus' religious opponents dragged this poor woman to Jesus in order to entrap him (John 8 in the KJV, RSV, and others). It was an ingenious plan, because Jesus would be howlingly wrong with either choice they presented him. They reminded Jesus that scripture commanded that she should be stoned: "Now in the law Moses commanded us to stone such. What do you say about her?"

They had Jesus on the horns of a delicious dilemma. If he said, "Yes. Stone her!" they would have accused him of being barbaric, fanatical, and outside the current moral and legal code because their idea of "right" had changed. However, if Jesus had said, "Are you kidding? That teaching of scripture fell out of practice long ago!" they could accuse him of rejecting both scripture and ancient tradition. They could say that he taught people to disregard and break the clear teaching of scripture. These "kind and righteous" religious leaders thought they had Jesus in an inescapable lose/lose situation. They were not interested in true righteousness; they were interested in being right. But we must remember that they also thought they were pleasing God and defending God's preferred will through their myopic cunning.

You already know Jesus' famous response: "Let him who is without sin among you be the first to throw a stone at her." Beginning with the oldest, the opponents all left. When they had gone, Jesus said, "Woman, where are they? Has no one condemned you? She said, "No one, Lord." And Jesus said, "Neither do I condemn you; go, and do not sin again." (John 8:7-11 selected, RSV). By doing this, Jesus simply deleted the clear words of scripture (Leviticus 20:10 and Deuteronomy 22:22) which commanded that adulterers be executed. He simply deleted them. They were morally wrong and outdated and he deleted them. Here, Jesus defied scripture but not tradition, because it was no longer the norm to execute adulterers.

Let's look next at Jesus' reinterpretation of the Sabbath. Sabbath observance was one of the most important aspects of Jewishness. Nevertheless, in his reinterpretation of Sabbath law, Jesus broke with both scripture and the contemporary traditional norms. It was one of the Ten Commandments, and scripture commanded death for those who failed to observe the Sabbath for infractions as minor as picking up sticks (Exodus 31:14, Numbers 15:32-36). It should be noted that many Old Testament scholars have concluded that the death sentence for moral infractions such as adultery or Sabbath breaking was seldom carried out; rather it was seen as an extreme upper limit of punishment, but this itself is a reinterpretation of scripture by the Jewish leadership by changing "must" to "may." That is a big difference.

The Jewish establishment viewed Sabbath observance primarily as an act of obedience to a divine command, and in Jesus' day the Pharisees seemed more concerned about keeping the letter of the law than they were about the spirit of it. Jesus confounded them all when he kept teaching that Sabbath observance which gets in the way of human well-being is not God's way. He repeatedly healed on the Sabbath, which was viewed as work and therefore as "Sabbath-breaking." Jesus also allowed his disciples to snap heads of grain and eat them on the Sabbath, which was viewed as Sabbath-breaking work. He scandalized the establishment when he declared that he was Lord of the Sabbath, and that the Sabbath was made for people rather than vice versa. In this one teaching, Jesus upended the Jewish theological understanding of Sabbath in both scripture and tradition.

Let's make a few applications here. First, we see that as early as the time of Jesus, the Jewish community itself had made adjustments to the teachings and commands of scripture. Often, the death penalty was not imposed upon Sabbath breakers or upon adulterers, although scripture commanded this. This is because some commandments and teachings that had been appropriate for the early Israelites in the desert were not regarded in the same light a thousand years later. The point here is that the moral teachings and commands of scripture have never been static. Second, we see that Jesus himself reinterpreted or eliminated scripture when it no longer fit the moral requirements of the day. These two observations are important because they tell us conservatives something about the nature of scripture.

Sometimes we can easily, but mistakenly, assume that the entirety of scripture is a kind of "one size fits all" proposition. That is, we might assume that all scripture is always meant to be applied in the same way across all contexts and times. That is simply not true, not just in one or two instances, but in a multitude of passages. If you doubt this, please re-read Leviticus or I Corinthians and consider how strange it would be to obey every law and teaching you find there. You will soon see what I mean. In case anyone is tempted to think,

"Well, it is only the Old Testament after all" I would remind you that when the writer of II Timothy 3:16,17 wrote, **"All scripture is inspired by God and is useful for teaching, for reproof, for correction, and for training in righteousness, so that everyone who belongs to God may be proficient, equipped for every good work,"** he was referring precisely and at that point, exclusively, to the Old Testament. There was no "New Testament" at that time. My point is that the interpretation and application of scripture, and our understanding of it, have always been updated from time to time. The ancient Jews did it, Jesus himself did it, and as we move along with our inquiry we will see that the Church has done it many, many times.

Of course, someone might very well object, "Jesus has unique authority to reinterpret scripture." I think both conservatives and progressives would agree with that statement. Jesus is Lord! His teachings are uniquely authoritative. And yet, if

> If scripture is statically perfect and unchanging, why did it need changing or reinterpreting by anyone, including Jesus?

Jesus felt the need to reinterpret scripture, that tells us something important about the nature of scripture. It is not monolithic. It is not static. Some of it is culture bound. If scripture is statically perfect and unchanging, why did it need changing or reinterpreting by anyone, including Jesus? The truth is, the interpretation and application of scripture is constantly updated through the centuries, but we conservatives drag our feet. Of course, we are supposed to resist change because we are conservative!

The story of the adulterous woman turns upon this very question. The reason the Pharisees posed this dilemma for Jesus is that the interpretation and application of the Mosaic law to stone adulterers was crystal clear in statement, but had always been extremely ambiguous in application. That ambiguity had become even greater with the passage of time and the imposition of Roman law. Everyone knew the clear teaching of scripture, both in Deuteronomy 22 and Leviticus 20, to stone adulterers. Everyone also knew that this teaching had never been systematically followed. Like the sodomy laws discussed in Chapter One, the law for stoning adulterers was "more honor'd in the breach." The ambiguity of applying clear scriptural teaching from a thousand years earlier was why the Pharisees saw this as a fitting trap for Jesus.

Go And Sin No More

My conservative friends may be thinking, "John, I'm so glad you brought this up. This story perfectly expresses my idea towards homosexuals: 'Neither do I condemn you. Go and sin no more.'" That is, if homosexuals will repent, God will forgive and redeem. This is essentially the stance discussed in Chapter One which the majority of gracious Christians embraced a few decades ago. I would agree with my conservative friends except for the fact that being LGBTQI is not a sin. It is like being born green-eyed or left handed. It may be different from the majority, but it is not a sin. The sin is how LGBTQI people are treated by many of us Christians. The sin is rejection. The sin is hell talk and hate talk. The sin is shaming. The sin is treating homosexuals as though they were "less than" heterosexuals. So I say to my conservative friends, "Go and sin no more. Repent of treating LGBTQI people as 'less than' just because they aren't heterosexual. Love and celebrate them as the wonderful LGBTQI people they are. God does."

By the way, this raises the question of "celebrating" homosexuality. Many conservatives feel they are conceding a great deal just to accept homosexuals; the idea of celebrating homosexuality seems to take things too far. "After all," conservatives might object, "why should homosexuality be celebrated any more than heterosexuality? I don't see heterosexuality being celebrated anywhere!" My response is, "Really? You don't think heterosexuality is celebrated? Then what are all those romantic movies, novels, and love songs about, if not celebrating heterosexual love?"

Authority to Accept and Bless

The Lord Jesus has given the Church enormous authority, more than we sometimes realize. We should appropriate this authority in the struggle to recognize LGBTQI people as full members of the family of faith. Jesus has given us authority to interpret and apply scripture. Scripture is a gift of God to the Church, from within the womb of the Church. The New Testament arose within the Church, and was recognized by the Church as authoritative. The Church alone has the right and responsibility to interpret scripture to the present age. Jesus has also told us that he will give us the Holy Spirit who will continue to guide us into all truth as the ages unfold (John 16:13). That is, Lowell's declaration that "time makes ancient good uncouth" might be more accurately stated as, "with time, the Holy Spirit reveals the love of God and neighbor more and more fully." Jesus went so far as to say to the Church: "Truly I tell you, whatever you bind on earth will be bound in heaven, and whatever you loose on earth will be loosed in heaven" (Matthew 18:18 NIV). This means that we, the Church, have authority to bind and loose, to approve or disapprove, to apply the love and truth of God to our changing world. The Lord respects us so much that he gives us this tremendous freedom to bless. It is okay to do what we think is right. We have our Lord's permission to move beyond the letter of the law into the spirit of grace, generosity and love. Let us bind bigotry, and loose love of neighbor!

Honoring Differing Views

You know where I stand on this issue. I hope that if you are a conservative open to a new perspective, we will find ourselves in agreement. But more importantly than that, I hope we can be forthright in acknowledging that people who sincerely love God and neighbor may honorably come to different conclusions about God's preferred will. We see multiple biblical examples of this tension between conservative and progressive interpretations of God's direction. The Christ event is the biggest example of this, in which the conservatives (Sadducees and Pharisees) rejected the progressive revelation that Jesus is the Christ. They also rejected the notion that Jesus had authority to reinterpret the laws of Moses and selectively ignore other religious laws that placed religious law above human welfare, as in the question about healing on the Sabbath. Conservative and progressive Christians in the

New Testament period also fought bitterly over the question of circumcision. These are just a few biblical examples of how conservatives and liberals who both claim to have the truth of God on their side can sincerely disagree. And as the saying goes, they should have learned how to disagree without being disagreeable, yet history is ablaze with the continuing saga of Christians disagreeing violently. The contemporary version of this

intolerant people of both sides cannot wait to demonstrate their supreme righteousness by ceasing communion with the "other."

hubris is one denominational split after another because of intolerant people on both sides of the question at hand, who cannot wait to demonstrate their supreme righteousness by ceasing communion with the "other." They usurp God's role of judgment and condemn their Christian sisters and brothers as "ungodly." Don't we view the breaking apart of the body of Christ as "ungodly?" Rather than seeking to break communion with those who read scripture differently, perhaps Christians should discern and honor the body of Christ by standing together in our diversity, united by unselfish love, as Paul urged the Corinthian Church (I Cor. 12-13). Sometimes ideas are most complete when held in tension with their opposites: law and grace, free will and predestination, death and eternal life. Treating Christians who differ from us with hatred, contempt, or pity is dishonest because it oversimplifies a complex problem, and it is un-Christlike because it demeans other members of Christ's body. It is better when conservatives and progressives in the body of Christ can see each other as complementary members of one body, each with valuable and honorable roles to play. As Paul writes, in I Cor. 12:12-14 (NIV): "Just as a body, though one, has many parts, but all its many parts form one body, so it is with Christ. For we were all baptized by one Spirit so as to form one body—whether Jews or Gentiles, slave or free—and we were all given the one Spirit to drink. Even so the body is not made up of one part but of many."

Questions for Reflection and Discussion

1. On E. M. Rogers' Diffusion of Innovation scale, from the beginning of the chapter, where would you put yourself with regard to homosexuality? Are you an early adopter, late adopter, etc.? How do you feel about that?

2. Research shows that the U.S. population, including most Christians, has passed the 50% tipping point in regard to the acceptance of homosexuality. Are you surprised in any way? Does this make you feel differently about your position? Why?

3. Do you think the Church's perception of "right" changes? If so, can you give a few examples? How do you feel about that?

4. The author asked, "If scripture is statically perfect and unchanging, why did it need changing or reinterpreting by anyone, including Jesus?" What is your response?

5. Jesus gives the Church the authority of binding and loosing. How should we use that authority in reference to our LGBTQI neighbors?

6. Do you find it hard to honor the views of Christians who differ from you on this subject? How do you see that in the light of scriptures which teach unity in the Church. In I Corinthians 1:10 (NRSV) we read, "Now I appeal to you, brothers and sisters, by the name of our Lord Jesus Christ, that all of you be in agreement and that there be no divisions among you, but that you be united in the same mind and the same purpose."

For Further Research: Do an internet search of scriptures about unity in the Church.

4

Blame the Holy Spirit!

I had Christian friends and loved ones who were gay, and so I knew about all the arguments. I had long ago heard the argument about the Holy Spirit leading the Church into further truth, but I always thought that was a very weak argument, because I did not believe the Holy Spirit would lead the Church into a new truth that was contrary to scripture. However, at that time, I did not fully appreciate the role that cultural conditioning played in the formation of scripture. Meanwhile, I met more and more homosexual people whose walk with the Lord I deeply respected. They passed the Acts 10 test (if God has given them the Holy Spirit, we must receive them into full fellowship).

Whenever I met a Christian whose faith I really respected, and who did not believe homosexuality was a sin, I would ask them to tell me about their faith journey. I would listen carefully, and challenge them when I disagreed with them. One day, I was talking to a pastor whose theology I deeply respected, and I asked her to explain how she dealt with the scriptures related to homosexuality. She said, "I set them aside." I could not believe my ears. I said, "you do what?" She said, "I set them aside, just as I set aside some other scriptures that are culture bound." It took me a year to think about this, but it began to make sense, especially when I thought about slavery in relation to scripture and tradition.

Last year, I was doing research on slavery and the oppression of black people in America. I was struck as never before by the fact that the writers of scripture were culturally conditioned to assume that slavery was both normal and morally acceptable. It took 1800 years for the Holy Spirit to convince the Church otherwise, despite plenty of scripture that supported the institution of slavery. The Church "set aside" the culturally conditioned scriptures that supported slavery. This new appreciation for the Holy Spirit's work in advancing righteousness contrary to scripture caused me to suspect that a similar combination of cultural conditioning and Holy Spirit inspiration might be at work in the Church's changing views on homosexuality. Let's explore.

Similar Crises in Church History
I have recognized a fairly regular pattern in Church history. There is the "normal" conservative position which is challenged by a more progressive

position. This progressive position opens the door to greater inclusion, recognizing that the "other" is fully human, and as such is invited to participate fully in the life and community of the Church. The conservatives compete with the

> *...conservatives compete with progressives, quoting scripture and tradition as they seek to keep the "other" clearly defined and subordinate.*

progressives, quoting scripture and tradition as they seek to keep the "other" clearly defined and subordinate. The first time this happened was straight out of the gate in the first century as the Jewish Christians wrestled with the challenge of Gentile inclusion.

The Gentile Problem

<u>Table Fellowship</u>

In Acts 10 we find the famous story of Peter and Cornelius. Cornelius was a Gentile. Although he had not converted to Judaism, he was a "God-fearer." This means he worshipped God and participated in certain Jewish ceremonies and traditions. As a captain in the Roman army, he was a generous and powerful supporter of the local Jewish community. An angel of God personally recruited Cornelius to become a Christian, and in a vision, the Holy Spirit instructed Peter to receive and evangelize him. What we sometimes miss is that the reason God had to speak to Peter so miraculously was to convince him and the early Church that it was actually God's will to receive and convert Gentiles. We may think this is a lovely story, and it is. But Peter and the early Church thought it was problematic. We can blame the Holy Spirit for these troubles.

The book of Acts is in many ways a record of the Holy Spirit at work in the early Church to evangelize the world. Since "the world" was mostly Gentile and the first Christians were Jewish, there was an immediate culture clash. It was ugly. Do you think the Lord knew it would be this way? Undoubtedly. And yet he plunged the first century Church into this ungainly fit of glorious growth anyway. Call it growing pains, because there is a lot that is both glorious and gross about a growth spurt.

All of us know that the earliest followers of Jesus were Jewish. We also know that almost immediately, Gentiles were attracted to the gospel. As we look back on this, it seems utterly natural, but it did not feel at all natural to the early Church.

It felt very unnatural for them to "set aside" scripture and tradition in this regard. The attraction of Gentiles to the Church raised immediate problems that were basic to scripture, tradition, and Christian identity: must Gentile converts become Jewish in order to become true Christians? Would they have table fellowship (eat together)? Would the Gentile Christians be accepted on equal footing with the Jewish Christians? What about circumcision?

Most of us today think the answers to these questions are pretty obvious. "No, you do not need to become Jewish in order to become authentically Christian. Yes, table fellowship with all Christians is at the heart of the gospel (even though some denominations still haven't figured this out). Yes, Christians of all ethnic groups are equally valued. No, circumcision is not a religious rite for most Christians, although many practice it." See? Easy.

But for the early Church, none of this was easy. This is partly because these questions cut to the heart of scripture and tradition for the earliest Jewish Christians. First century Jewish Christians were initially seen as a sect of Judaism, and it took time for them to develop a distinctive identity apart from simply being Jews who believed Jesus to be the Messiah. What we now call the Old Testament was scripture for both Judaism and early Christianity, and although the Church gradually developed the New Testament, this took many years. So the teachings of the Old Testament and the rituals and values of first century Judaism were part of the religious identity and values of the early Jewish Christians. For that reason, the admission of Gentiles into the Church was an enormous problem. These Gentile converts knew next to nothing about Jewish scripture, culture or religious practices. Nor were they particularly interested.

In addition, many Jewish Christians wanted absolutely nothing to do with Gentiles- converted or not- because Gentiles were firmly "other." Gentiles were not their social equals, nor did they feel comfortable with the suggestion that they should become so. The scripture and Jewish tradition were brimming with social and religious barriers between Jews and Gentiles; to expect the earliest Jewish Christians to "just get over it" would be unrealistic.

This is precisely what the unseemly scene at Antioch was about, as recorded in Galatians 2. Recall that Paul, who had converted to become the uber-progressive in this story, had received a call from God to evangelize the Gentiles. Recall also that in about 50 A.D. he had traveled to Jerusalem and conferred with the leaders of the Jerusalem

Church (the Jewish Christians) about this mission. This was called the First Jerusalem Council. The Council had approved Paul's mission to the Gentiles, and with great difficulty they had modified the requirements of becoming a Christian so that Gentiles were not bound by most of the law of Moses, including male circumcision. They were to remember the poor, and according to Acts 15:29 (NRSV) "abstain from what has been sacrificed to idols and from blood and from what is strangled and from fornication." This was very difficult for the Jerusalem Church, but they were able to stretch that far, again, contrary to scripture and tradition. Peter, James, and John shook on the deal with Paul, offering him the "right hand of fellowship." But things went south in a hurry.

In Antioch, one of the first Christian churches outside Jerusalem, there were both Jewish and Gentile Christians. Paul was there when Peter came to visit. Apparently, Peter was in his glory, enjoying wonderful Christian fellowship and the beautiful way that the dividing walls between Jews and Gentiles had been broken down in Christ Jesus. Specifically, Peter had table fellowship with the Gentile Christians. This was extremely controversial, but it seemed eminently appropriate to the adventuresome Peter who had a direct revelation from God about this very matter. . .until men from the Jerusalem Church came to "infiltrate and spy" on their freedom. Apparently these spies sent a damning report to Jerusalem, and James sent men to Antioch to bring him back a first-hand report. When the men from James arrived, Peter withdrew from table fellowship with the Gentiles. When Paul noticed what Peter was doing, he precipitated a public showdown with Peter about his vacillation. Peter was the moderate caught between the conservative block led by James and the progressive block led by Paul.

Do you hear what is going on? Infiltration? Spies? Public arguments? Yes, this is the Church having growing pains, and the issue was table fellowship. The conservatives had stretched as far as they could. Indeed, they had stretched so far at the Jerusalem Council that they could not comfortably stand by their word. And although the conservatives were some of the most highly respected people in all the Church, they came to be viewed by many among posterity as remarkably small, ugly, and mean spirited. The ground was shifting under their feet, and they could not regain their footing. They could not envision a Christianity that truly included Gentiles as equal members. For them, Gentiles, even those who had accepted Christ, would always be "other" and "less than." Table fellowship was absolutely out of the question, kind of like the ordination of LBGTQI Christians is out of the question for some today.

After all, what if a homosexual presided at the communion table of Christian sacrament and fellowship?

Circumcision

Table fellowship was an important issue for the early Church. Circumcision was a separate but related issue of even more importance. The circumcision controversy is germane to our discussion for three reasons: circumcision was clearly commanded by scripture, it was a widely accepted tradition practiced for more than a thousand years, and the decision to step away from it was highly controversial. Genesis 17 makes it clear that male circumcision is the outward and visible sign of the covenant made between God, Abraham, and all Abraham's male descendants forever. Many other scripture passages reiterate the central importance of this rite. It was one of the greatest distinguishing characteristics between those who were members of the covenant relationship, and those who were not. It was extraordinarily difficult for the Jerusalem Council to decide not to require circumcision. As it turns out, this was not a decision all the important leaders agreed on, and the aftershocks of this decision roiled the Church for years afterward.

Circumcision was an enormous deterrent to evangelism. Not only was this a painful operation which few grown men would have embraced, but according to the Hellenistic esthetic standards of the day it would have mutilated the beauty of the male figure. In terms of the image of wheat used earlier, Paul and many others saw circumcision as part of the husk of the gospel. James and his group saw it as part of the kernel. The Judaizers believed that if a man truly wanted to become a Christian, he should willingly accept this rite of initiation, which they viewed as central to initiation into the Christian community. They further believed that those who were unwilling to give up their prerogative on this point were not worthy to be included among the faithful.

On the other hand, Paul and his progressive group spiritualized the concept of circumcision, as in Philippians 3:3. They believed in what John Wesley called the "circumcision of the heart," saying that the true children of God are those who are circumcised in heart and not merely in the flesh.

This was a battle that raged fiercely as Paul's people "set aside" the scriptures and tradition requiring circumcision. The entire book of Galatians revolves around the dispute between Paul and the Judaizers who taught that Gentile converts must adhere to Mosaic law- contrary to what was decided at the Jerusalem Council. Famously, Paul flares in anger: "I wish that the people who are upsetting you would go all the way; let them go on and castrate themselves!" (5:12, GNT). Another example is found in Philippians 3:2-3 (NIV): "Watch out for those dogs, those evildoers, those mutilators of the flesh. For it is we who are the circumcision, we who serve God by his Spirit, who boast in Christ Jesus, and who put no confidence in the flesh." In these contexts, Paul calls the Judaizers "dogs" and "evildoers" and sarcastically interjects that he wishes they would castrate themselves. You recognize that all these folks love Jesus, right?

You recognize that all these folks love Jesus, right?

Have you noticed that this is not nice? That is because it wasn't. It was white hot as the conservatives, who had the Jerusalem Church and a thousand years of scripture and tradition behind them, dug in against the progressives, who had the Spirit of the Lord behind them. Honestly, since I am a conservative, my heart goes out to them. They had every reason to believe they were doing the right thing. They had scripture and tradition on their side. But they were wrong. This controversy eventually faded. The Judaizers died out and the evangelizers pushed on. Eventually, it was no longer an issue and Christians in later generations wondered what the fuss had been about.

The Slavery Problem

It is embarrassingly true that both the Old Testament and the New Testament specifically and repeatedly support the institution of slavery, and nowhere in the Bible is it forbidden. There are far too many references to slaves and slavery in scripture to count or quote, because the institution of slavery is completely woven into the fabric of every ancient culture. In the culture of both the Old Testament and the New Testament periods, slavery was universally accepted as right, just and correct. Throughout these periods of history, there were different forms of slavery and there were different ways that people could become slaves. For example, people could become slaves because they were conquered by other nations, and they could also become slaves either to raise money (as in the case of a man selling his children or himself into slavery) or they could become enslaved as payment for debts. Several biblical passages regulate the institution of slavery, which is a clear way of supporting and refining the system. None call for its abolition.

The New Testament is no better than the Old in this regard. The Koine Greek word for slave can also be translated servant, and in modern translations this is now the norm. But be aware that in most cases where you see the word servant in English, the more accurate translation is "slave," because for the most part these "servants" weren't paid; they were owned. Slavery was simply the cultural norm and the Greek word "doulos" means "slave or servant." To be sure, there are a couple of passages which condemn slave traders who are assumed to kidnap vulnerable people and sell them into bondage, and Paul urges Philemon to accept the slave Onesimus as a brother in Christ; but you will notice that Paul still sends the slave back to his owner without calling for his legal manumission. In the New Testament, slaves are viewed as being spiritually free, but not legally free, and nowhere in the Bible is a call for abolition of slavery made. To the contrary, believing slaves are diligently instructed to obey their masters in order to please the Lord (Colossians 3:22, Ephesians 6:5, I Peter 2:18-20). This is one of the reasons slave-owners wanted their slaves to become Christians; it was a way of controlling them.

If the Scripture and tradition supported slavery, and they did, how did the Church lead the world in overthrowing the institution? What was their

scriptural support?
What was their moral
strength? How did
they "set aside" the
scripture and
tradition supporting
slavery?

The Holy Spirit
gradually stirred
minds and hearts to
see that slavery was
simply wrong in spite
of scriptural and
traditional support

The Holy Spirit stirred minds and hearts to see that slavery was wrong, in spite of scriptural and traditional support for the institution.

for the institution. By the guiding light of the Holy
Spirit, believers were led into a greater truth and
were given grace to see it clearly. Their scriptural
support was not found in the scriptures relating
directly to slavery, for those passages assumed the
moral rectitude of the institution and directly
supported it in many cases. Their scriptural
support was found in the broader, overarching
themes of scripture such as the Golden Rule (Luke
6:31) and the great, two-fold command (Mark
12:29-31). The abundant scriptural teachings of
love of neighbor were gradually seen as
overcoming and exceeding the culture bound
teachings concerning slavery. In addition, the
values of freedom and equality were culturally

ascendant in the late eighteenth century. These values are rooted in the Church and its scripture, and they gradually overtook the institution of slavery.

John Wesley had been a missionary to Georgia in 1736 and had seen first-hand the brutality of slavery. He and his friend George Whitefield were determined to do something to improve the condition and treatment of slaves. You will recognize this as the traditional approach of both scripture and the Church: advocating for better treatment of slaves without questioning or condemning the institution of slavery itself. Destruction of the institution had not crossed Wesley's mind until he read an account of slavery by the American Quaker, Anthony Benezet. Wesley was suddenly possessed by the idea that slavery was not to be improved, but abolished. This was a leap forward, past scripture as it had been previously interpreted, and past millennia of tradition, a leap that came from the inspiration of the Holy Spirit. Wesley began using his enormous influence to eliminate the trade. In fact, the last letter of his life was written to William Wilberforce, encouraging him to stay in the fight for the abolition of slavery. It took Wilberforce a lifetime, but the campaign he led resulted in the Slavery Abolition Act, which abolished slavery in most of the British Empire. Wilberforce learned that the act would pass just three days before his own death.

Americans know all too well that as the moral question of slavery was raised to the pitch of a rebel yell, Christ lovers on both sides of the Mason Dixon were quoting scripture and preparing for war. The conservatives claimed the authority of scripture and tradition, and they were manifestly correct in doing so. And yet, the moral ground was shifting beneath their feet. An institution which had seemed unassailably correct from earliest civilization was now under fire, literally. The progressives had gained an awareness of the evil of the institution, and they couldn't "unsee" it. They were determined to eradicate the practice.

Now that personal fortunes are no longer involved, we can all easily see that the Gospel's ethic of love prohibits the enslavement of others, despite the many individual culture bound scriptures that support the institution. This is a hugely important concept. Holy love of others causes us to "set aside" scripture and tradition contrary to it. Multiple scriptures relating specifically to slavery supported the institution in one way or another. Only the general, overarching teachings of the Golden Rule and the Great Commandment were able finally to stamp out the unjust treatment of slaves. Gradually, the "other" was recognized as brother and sister. The "other" was recognized as fully human and was welcomed as equal in the Church. It took a long time. Some would say we aren't there yet. Along that line, I wonder why so many churches still seem racially segregated, and why we see mostly black pastors pastoring black churches, and white pastors pastoring white churches?

The Sexism Problem

The sexism problem (prejudice or discrimination based on sex) is much like the slavery problem. Sexism was an unquestioned assumption of every culture, woven into the fabric of society at its most basic level. The writers of scripture certainly did not think to question it; they assumed it was right and good. They had no other lens through which to view gender and sexuality. Nor did they wish to infuriate Roman culture by radically changing the status of women.

In the very beginning of the Bible, we read the judgment upon Eve in Genesis 3:16 (NIV): "Your desire shall be for your husband, and he shall rule over you." This thread of men ruling over women is woven throughout the Bible, and throughout civilization. The idea does not originate with written scripture, since sexism certainly predates the writing of Genesis. This power differential, and hence sexism, was universally assumed to be natural, normal, and appropriate. The place of women in ancient societies such as Israel, Greece and Rome is both fascinating and appalling. There were differences among societies and among social classes, but extreme sexism was a given of all. Sexism is the unredeemed product of unequal power between men and women. It is not part of God's good plan for humanity. It is part of the "fall." It is a product of the sinfulness of humanity, a result of the curse which is proleptically reversed in the Second Adam, Jesus Christ.

Jesus actually treated women like "people." In Jesus' day, rabbis seldom spoke to women in public, but Jesus freely did. Women did not travel in the company of rabbis, but highly respected women traveled with Jesus' entourage, including Mary Magdalene, Joanna and Susanna (Luke 8:1-3). Women were not disciples of rabbis, but among the 70 disciples (a larger circle than the 12), several seem to have been women. One Patristic Era list includes Apphia and Junia as disciples. In addition, in Matthew 12:49-50 Jesus refers to his disciples and says, "here are my mother, and my brothers. For whoever does the will of my Father in heaven is my brother and sister and mother." Many see this as a clear indication that there were women in the larger group who were called disciples.

Women were not taught by rabbis, but Jesus was happy to teach both women and men. We also see women who were the last to leave the scene of the cross and first to the empty tomb. They were an integral part of the group of male disciples. In fact, there is a March 31, 2018 article in the *London Times* written by Kaya Burgess which headlines: "Half of Jesus' Disciples Were Women." The article may or may not be correct, but the place of women in the ministry of Jesus is appearing larger and larger with increasing research. Interestingly, Mark Allen Powell has a chart in his introduction to Luke's gospel which shows abundant male/female parallels. All of this seems quite normal to us, but to Jesus' contemporaries it was scandalous.

Like today, women also made up a majority of members of the early Church. Why? Because women were valued. They were given status and dignity within the Church as opposed to their ordinary cultural experience, and their gifts and abilities were seen as important. Although women were not allowed leadership in Jewish synagogues, women as well as men were leaders in the early Church. In Acts 18, we see that Priscilla and Aquila were co-founders of the church in Ephesus. In Romans 16:7 Paul names Junia and Andronicus as being outstanding among the apostles. That is huge. Junia is not only named as an apostle, she is named as an *outstanding* apostle. In Romans 16 other women, as well as men, are named as leaders in the Church: Mary, Tryphena, Tryphosa, Persis, Julia, and the sister of Nereus. In Philippians 4, Paul calls Euodia and Syntyche fellow workers in the gospel. There were also women who led house-churches: Apphia, Prisca, Lydia, and Nympha.

Equally important is the passage from I Cor. 11. This is an undisputed letter of Paul's in which he stipulates that women who pray and prophesy in Church must wear a head covering. The point he is trying to make is the importance of the head covering. But the point he makes indirectly is that women were exercising the office of prophet in the early Church, otherwise there would have been no need for his mentioning the head-covering. By the way, it is worth noting here that Paul's problem is not that women are exercising leadership in church, but that they are taking their freedom in Christ too far and abandoning their head coverings. Head coverings in that culture symbolized that the women were under the "covering" of their husbands. To throw off the head covering was suggestive of the appearance of being sexually available though married. This may not have been the women's intention, but Paul saw it as a step too far. Paul also objected to some of the women in the Corinthian church being disruptive during the service with their gossiping and chatter (the Greek word is "laleo" which means "chatter.") Paul does not object here to women *speaking* in worship (the Greek word for speaking is "lego") but to their disruptive *chatter* in worship.

Paul famously celebrated in Galatians 3:28 (NIV), "There is neither Jew nor Gentile, neither slave nor free, nor is there male and female, for you are all one in Christ Jesus." This may be the high water mark for freedom and the breaking down of cultural divisions in the early Church. It was a moment of great clarity in which Paul prophetically called for the walls of division to come down. It was a prophetic and proleptic flash of the kingdom of God among us. It was also short-lived.

By 64 A.D., the Emperor Nero started the first persecution of the Christians. At about the same time, we observe a change in the early Church; it seems to become more concerned with appearing to conform to social norms. Church leadership and Church teaching seems to become increasingly hierarchical and male-dominated, in conformity with Roman social mores. In these slightly later letters such as Colossians, we still see the grace of Christ at work, but it seems to be operating within a slightly tighter framework. Teaching that seems to subordinate or silence women emerges at this point. I Timothy 2:12 says, "And I do not permit a woman to teach or to have authority over a man, but to be in silence." Instead of proclaiming no barriers between Jew, Gentile, slave, free, male or female, slaves are instructed to obey their masters and wives their husbands. Tempering this, however, is the teaching that husbands are instructed to love their wives as Christ loves the Church, and not to be harsh. There is a mutuality here which is a beautiful new teaching, but it seems to fall short of the rapturous vision of Galatians 3. Gradually, the curtain comes down and the Church becomes more hierarchical and more sexist, like the culture. The Church was certainly progressive in its teachings of treating everyone including women and slaves with justice, kindness, compassion, and love, but the early spark of gender equality seems to have become more regulated.

This kind of traditional, fallen sexism became the norm for nearly two thousand years. For example, under English common law, a woman was legally considered her husband's chattel. This was derived from the legal doctrine of coverture, in which a woman was considered to be under her husband's protection and legal authority. This began to change in the nineteenth century, but in America women only got the legal right to vote in 1920. It was also very difficult for women to gain the freedom to choose a profession.

One of the last bastions of sexism in the workplace had to do with the ordination of women to become priests or pastors. This was because scripture and tradition were on the side of conservatives who quoted those few New Testament passages declaring that women should remain silent in the Church, and they should not be given authority to teach men. There are still some denominations that teach this. For example, women cannot be ordained Roman Catholic Priests. Also, many Baptist churches require that women leaders have authority only over other women and that these female leaders remain under the ultimate authority of a male leader.

Through the work of the Holy Spirit, many Christians have realized that this is simply wrong, and so we "set aside" those scriptures as culturally conditioned. A male dominated social and ecclesiastical structure may have been appropriate in the first century, but once again, "time makes ancient good uncouth." The ancient legal doctrine of coverture, which was constructed to protect women, eventually ceased to make their lives better and instead became a suffocating legal straight jacket. Gradually, people realized that women are fully human! Gradually, people realized that women should have the same rights and opportunities as men. Gradually, people realized that it was time to outgrow the cultural husk of the Bible's teaching concerning the submission of women. I Timothy 2:12, I Corinthians 14:33-35, Titus 2:3-5, Ephesians 5:22, and I Peter 3:1 are all scriptures that reiterate the traditional view of women's relationships with men. This cultural view which was traditional and dominant during the first century required repeated reinforcement in scripture passages because, through the good news of the gospel, the Holy Spirit was breaking the stronghold of women's oppression.

I realize there are many Christians who still believe that sexism is God's will, and that the above mentioned scriptures are God's kernel of eternal truth rather than the cultural husk which carries God's truth. But for those of us who believe that sexism is wrong, and that women should be able to speak in church, teach men, or be ordained, for us, this is another example of scripture and tradition which needed to be "set aside," and which the Holy Spirit has helped us to outgrow. Instead, we have chosen to focus on the scriptures which celebrate the ministerial roles of women which were cited above, and which also include the visionary passage from Joel which is quoted in Acts 2:17 (NIV): "In the last days, God says, I will pour out my Spirit on all people. Your sons and daughters will prophesy, your young men will see visions, and your old men will dream dreams."

Conclusion

Certain teachings of scripture are culture bound and when the time is right, we set them aside. Was it ever God's will to tell women to be silent in church, or is that just something that the Church got wrong because the influence of a sexist culture was so pervasive that the writers of scripture and the Church could not hear the Holy Spirit speaking anything to the contrary? I don't know. But I am pretty sure that the Holy Spirit has led the Church to understand that women are fully human, and not somehow subordinate to men.

Was slavery ever pleasing to God? No, but it was so culturally entrenched that it was normalized by the writers of scripture. They thought they were doing God's will when they tried to make the institution more just. It took two thousand years for Jesus' message to penetrate the heart of the Church and the culture. Then suddenly, the "slavery" scriptures were just set aside in favor of the "love" scriptures.

God does not just drop a perfect paradigm upon society and bring the heavenly kingdom upon earth in one moment, with all its values manifested monolithically and instantaneously.

Instead, God gradually and progressively reveals to us his will and his values as the Holy Spirit leads us into fuller truth, just as Jesus promised (John 16:13). God's truth can be summed up in the Great Commandment to love God supremely and neighbor as self, but it is taking millennia for us to apply that to every area of life. Cultural prejudice, pride, exploitation and exclusion are difficult to pin down and devilishly elusive. But they are gradually overcome by the gospel; sometimes in slow and incremental steps, and at other times in great leaps. Concerning LGBTQI people, the Church is taking another great leap, just as we did with Gentiles, slaves, and women.

But Gentiles, slaves and women have something important in common: they did not *choose* to be "that way." They were born that way. Are LGBTQI people born that way?

Questions for Reflection and Discussion

1. What do you think of how James, Paul and Peter behaved concerning the controversy at Antioch? (Galatians 2:11-14)

2. Concerning Gentile inclusion, who were the early adopters, and who were the late adopters? Do you think the first generation of the Jerusalem Church ever fully accepted Gentiles? Why?

3. Conservative, Progressive, Moderate- which one are you on the LGBTQI issue? How does that feel?

4. What was the role of the Holy Spirit as the early Church sorted through problems of Gentile inclusion?

5. How important was circumcision to the early Jewish Church? Why? How do you think they felt about dropping it as a requirement for Gentiles? Do you think everyone was on board with this?

6. Concerning circumcision, Paul and his followers saw it as the "husk" of the gospel. The Judaizers saw it as the "kernel" of the gospel and felt that if the Gentiles were sincere they would be willing to undergo circumcision. Is this at all analogous to our challenge of including LGBTQI people? Are there some who believe that LGBTQI people who want to convert should be willing to give up their sexual identity to do so? Is this even possible? Would they be accepted on an equal footing with heterosexuals?

7. In what ways did scripture give support to the institution of slavery? In what ways was scripture used to dismantle slavery? Why do you think the writers of scripture didn't

just come out and directly call for the abolition of slavery?

8. Who had scripture and tradition on their side in the slavery debates? In the debates about sexism? Which scriptures are the most important?

9. What if the Church today held onto traditional ideas of sexism as laid out in scripture and tradition? Would you want to be part of a Church like that? Would you leave, or would you work from within to change the system?

For Further Research: Do an internet search about circumcision in the early Church. Think about why the Judaizers were convinced they were right. How did the Church move beyond them?

5

Born That Way?

There is a couple in my congregation who are here only for a brief time each summer, but they share a deep interest with me in the welfare of orphans in Rwanda. On that basis, we get together for lunch and fellowship. Last year as we were finishing up our

> *If people are born "that way" God made them that way. And "God don't make no junk."*

shrimp and grits at a local restaurant, Greg shared with me some of the amazing research that was coming out about the genetic factors concerning homosexuality. He had written extensively on the subject and shared his work with me. Until this time, I had been aware of no credible research linking genetics and homosexuality. This information was a game changer for me. If people are born "that way" then that means God made them that way. And as they say, "God don't make no junk."

What Does LGBTQI Mean?

This is Greg speaking. I will be writing about the science of homosexuality. Human sexuality used to be a bipolar world: one was either heterosexual or homosexual. But then, as we paid closer attention, it became clearer and clearer that there were more distinctions—way more distinctions. Each has its own name, and the first letter of each became part of the shorthand for some of the array of "non-heterosexual" orientation—not just homosexual, because other options may not involve same-sex attraction. We use six letters in this book: LGBTQI, although there are many others as well. Simplistically, here is what they signify:

> L: Lesbian – a woman who is sexually attracted to women.
>
> G: Gay – a man who is sexually attracted to men.
>
> B: Bisexual – a man or woman who is sexually attracted to men and women.
>
> T: Transgender – individuals whose physical sexual characteristics at birth differ from their gender identity. A person whose anatomy is male at birth but who identifies as a female is a trans woman. A person

whose anatomy is female at birth but who identifies as a male is a trans man.

Q: Queer or Questioning – a man or woman who does not identify as gay, lesbian, bi or straight, transgender or cisgender, or who is in the process of sorting out his or her orientation or gender identity.

I: Intersex – a person whose anatomy at birth is neither male nor female or both male and female, running the spectrum from undeveloped or underdeveloped sexual organs on the one hand, to both male and female sexual organs on the other.

The most important thing to understand about human sexuality—and one can appreciate this just from the definitions above—is that it is complex. Very complex. It consists essentially of two parts: sexual orientation, which is defined by the person to whom one is attracted (which can include sexual, emotional, social, romantic and spiritual attraction); and gender identity, which is how one self-identifies. Gender identity is different from sexual orientation. Sexual orientation is defined by the person you go to bed *with*, and gender identity is defined by the person you go to bed *as*.

Picture a matrix with four boxes. One axis is sexual orientation, which may be heterosexual, homosexual, bisexual, or other; and the other axis is gender identity, which may be cis-gender (in which one's identity matches one's anatomical sex), or transgender (in which they do not match). The boxes represent the possible combinations. But, in reality, there are many more for each axis, and so the number of possible combinations is very large. For the purpose of simplicity, with due respect to the diversity of terms, this chapter will deal mostly with homosexuality, and mostly with the male version of homosexuality, for the reason that this is where science has spoken most clearly —thus far.

Homosexuality is Complex

Seven decades ago, when Alfred Kinsey brought the study of human sexuality into the daylight, he placed it on a scale from 0—completely heterosexual—to 6—completely homosexual—with a score of 3 denoting bisexuality. Although Kinsey's scale moved understanding forward in the short term, it worked against it in the long term for two reasons. First, it described only one side of the coin: sexual orientation. It said nothing about gender identity. Second, by placing various embodiments of sexual orientation on a single straight-line scale, it suggested that while different sexual orientations may vary from each other quantitatively, they were qualitatively the same. But they are not. Indeed, male homosexuality is not simply the mirror image of female homosexuality. A special issue of *National Geographic* in January of 2017, entitled "Gender Revolution," notes that Facebook offers users fifty terms to characterize their sexuality. Rather than viewing sexuality linearly, one should imagine a multi-dimensional array—something like a galaxy of stars with clusters in some locations, single stars in others, and empty space in between. If you can construct that mental image, you have some appreciation for the complexity of human sexuality in all of its flavors—heterosexuality included—and also can appreciate that the search for a single cause of all homosexuality is as fruitless as the quest for the Holy Grail.

Biology

"Born that way" has long been a self-identifier within LGBTQI communities. For many, there was not a time in life where they did not identify as LGBTQI. Much of the strength within the gay rights movement has evolved through the emergence, from the shadows, of this self-

Policy was informed by dogma, not data.

realization. Earlier societal norms were so strong that they not only enabled most straight people to see homosexuality as chosen and sinful, but also forced many LGBTQI persons to view themselves as sinners, even as they struggled with the reality that their sexual orientation and gender identity were not choices.

Science had little to say in the 1970s about the nature of homosexuality. Policy was informed by dogma, not data. When I was doing doctoral studies in pathology at UCLA from 1973 to 1975, there was not yet a graduate course offered there in the nascent field of molecular biology—and molecular biology has been the key to the scientific understanding of homosexuality.

As the field matured and the sequencing of genes became routine, the hunt for the "gay gene" was on. The assumption was that homosexuality, like many physical traits such as eye and hair color, was determined by one gene. As it gradually became apparent that there was no gay gene, behaviorists began to proclaim victory; but in fact, science hadn't even begun to speak. What follows is a summary of how science has informed us about homosexuality. I write this as a scientist who has spent over four decades in biomedical research. Bear in mind that what I will describe is an ongoing journey and not a destination. This is very much an interim report.

Prevalence of Homosexuality

There is a general consensus that between 2.5% and 5% of adults throughout the world self-identify as gay, lesbian or bisexual. There is no persuasive evidence that the percentage has varied significantly across time or geography. Long-term same-sex pair bonding has been reported in ungulates and some birds. A well-documented study of sheep showed that, given a choice, 8% of rams mated exclusively with other rams. A standard reference on the subject of homosexuality in animals, published in 1999, documents homosexual behavior in nearly 500 species of animals,[1] while an estimate seven years later put the number at 1,500.

Genetics

Two kinds of biological mechanisms shape sexuality, whether heterosexual or homosexual: genetics and epigenetics. *Genetics* refers to DNA. Think of DNA as a long strand of beads of just four colors. Human cells contain 46 chromosomes, each of which is a very long strand of those beads. Within each strand are more than a thousand

---

[1] Bruce Bagemihl, *Biological Exuberance: Animal Homosexuality and Natural Diversity* (New York: St. Martin's Press, 1999).

genes. *Epigenetics* refers to processes that can influence the manner in which genes do their thing. As an analogy, think of genetics as the blueprint for building a home, and epigenetics as the tools in a general contractor's toolkit that allow him or her to make on-site alterations that determine how the final house appears.

Some of the earliest clues to the biology of homosexuality came from the study of twins. Monozygotic ("one egg," or identical) twins come from a single fertilized egg that splits into two shortly after fertilization, with the two eggs—and the subsequent twins—having identical DNA. Dizygotic ("two eggs," or fraternal) twins result from simultaneous fertilization of two eggs whose DNA may match each other by as little as 50%. If genetics were the only factor underlying homosexuality, one would expect 100% concordance among identical twins—that is, both twins would either be heterosexual or homosexual. If genetics were not a factor at all, one would expect the same concordance among fraternal twins as among identical twins.

In fact, the numbers fall between the two extremes. One major study of male twins showed the concordance rate among identical twins to be 52%, but only 22% among fraternal twins. The study also looked at non-twin biological brothers, and found a concordance rate of only 9%. Thus, a single study provided strong evidence both for a role of genetics in determining sexuality—the concordance being more than double in monozygotic twins than in dizygotic—and for a role of epigenetics—the concordance being more than double in dizygotic twins than in non-twin biological brothers. In other words, the conditions within the womb can vary from one pregnancy to another in the same mother, with markedly different results.

Subsequent studies have shown that the DNA methylation profile—that is, molecules attached to portions of DNA that strongly affect the manner in which the DNA is regulated—is not identical between monozygotic twins at the time of birth, even though they have the same DNA. Thus, one identical twin may be gay while the other is straight, in spite of them having identical DNA. Identical twins are not as identical as we once supposed.

At the level of DNA, variations specific genes in the X chromosome and chromosomes 7, 8 and 10 appear more frequently in homosexual men. However, no cause-and-effect relationship has yet been established. In other words, there still is no such thing as a "gay gene."

While anatomical sex generally is determined genetically—people with two X-chromosomes will be anatomically female, while those with one X- and one Y-chromosome will be anatomically male —sexual orientation and gender identity are largely determined by hormones. In humans, the primary hormone is testosterone. Several well-characterized naturally occurring or induced conditions involving hormones are known to influence, on a permanent basis, sexual orientation in a direction different than anatomical sex: androgen insensitivity syndrome, 5α-reductase deficiency, 17β-hydroxysteroid dehydrogenase deficiency, congenital adrenal hyperplasia, and prenatal exposure to physician-prescribed hormones. The names are tongue twisting, but the take-home message is that each operates through a different biological mechanism, and likely results in a different "flavor" of homosexuality. All are permanent.

Epigenetics

While genetics is a factor, it is not the only factor that determines sexual orientation. The other, and more dominant factor is epigenetics. From the time the fertilized egg is implanted in the wall of the uterus until birth, the developing fetus is immersed—literally—in a sea of maternal factors that help to shape its development. Sometimes, epigenetics can take the fetus down a different pathway than the genetic code prescribes. I will walk you through two important examples of how epigenetics can shift sexual orientation towards homosexuality.

The first is the birth-order effect, which is seen only in males. It is estimated that 15% to 28% of gay men owe their sexual orientation to this effect. While the mechanism is not completely understood, it appears to be due to interactions between the male fetus and the maternal immune system that have increased consequences for each subsequent male birth. After the birth of one son the likelihood of each subsequent son of the same biological mother being gay increases by 33%. If the likelihood of the first is 3%, then that of the second is 4%. The effect is additive, such that the seventh son would have a 17% chance of being gay. Daughters do not experience a similar phenomenon, nor is the effect on sons influenced by the number of older sisters. And the effect is only true for right-handed sons. It is, indeed, complicated.

The other example is probably more important in causing homosexuality. It is called "epigenetically canalized sexual development." In plainer English, at a very early stage of fetal development, epigenetic factors that are not part of the DNA but can be passed from either parent to the fetus affect the way the "sex" of the fetal brain is imprinted. What that means is this: testosterone is present in all developing fetuses, but in higher levels in the male. However, in order for testosterone to exert its effect in imprinting maleness into the fetal brain, there must be a receptor for it within that brain. (Think of the process as a series of locked doors, which are analogous to testosterone receptors; and keys, which are analogous to testosterone. A disparity either in the number of doors or the number of keys will affect the number of doors that can be *opened*.) Generally, male fetuses have higher levels of testosterone *and* higher levels of testosterone receptors, while females have lower levels of testosterone *and* lower levels of testosterone receptors.

In some instances, however, there is a mismatch that is determined by an epigenetic factor that may be inherited from a parent. This can result in male embryos with low levels of receptors, in which case testosterone cannot exert its masculinizing effect on the brain. Alternatively, female embryos can have high levels of receptors, in which case even the normally low testosterone levels that circulate within the blood of female fetuses are preferentially grabbed by those receptors, thus exerting a masculinizing effect on the brain.

All of this brain imprinting occurs prenatally. At the time of puberty, when testosterone or estrogen levels begin to spike, the imprinted brain is impervious to their effect, notwithstanding the gender of the genitalia. In other words, a female with a fetal-masculinized brain will be sexually oriented towards women; while a male with a fetal-feminized brain will be sexually oriented towards men, hormones—and hormone therapy—notwithstanding.

The percentage of homosexual men in gay-tolerant societies is no higher than in gay- averse societies.

Since these epigenetic factors are not necessarily inherited equally, one identical twin may be gay while the other is straight, in spite of them having identical DNA. This is yet another example of identical twins not being as identical as we once supposed.

The genesis of sexual orientation is an area of science that is undergoing much cutting-edge research, and it is certain that future discoveries will elucidate more examples of homosexuality being biologically determined, whether through genetics, epigenetics, or a combination. But the bottom line has already been written: homosexuals are, indeed, "born that way."

Choice

Let's take a moment to look at the assertion that homosexuality is merely a choice, rather than a biological imprint. While it is documented that homosexual behavior increases when the opposite sex is absent—think of prisons or unisex schools—such behavior is transient, and upon reentering the larger society these people resume their heterosexual orientation, never having abandoned it. Even in societies such as New Guinea, where adolescent male homosexual behavior is encouraged as a means to preserve female virginity until marriage, adult males show no higher incidence of homosexuality than those in non-permissive cultures. The percentage of homosexual men in gay-tolerant societies such as Thailand and the Philippines is no higher than in gay-averse societies. Currently available scientific studies show little or no influence of education in determining sexual orientation. And finally, children raised by homosexual parents are no more likely to become homosexual than children raised by heterosexual parents. To quote a prominent expert, "No theories that attribute the development of homosexuality to non-biological causes have produced convincing data to support their interpretations. If *any* role of social and educational factors exists, that it so far has escaped a rigorous demonstration strongly suggests that these roles are severely limited."[2]

The biology described in this chapter represents the best-defined areas of research into human sexuality, but not the only research. We may expect new insights into the biological underpinnings of homosexuality in its various "flavors" as science continues to probe. For now, the essential points to bear in mind are these:

- Human sexuality is complex and far from "bipolar." Even within each of the two general categories of sexual orientation and gender identity, there are many flavors. The combinations of flavors are almost limitless, and it is likely that most eventually will be found to have unique biological origins.

- Within the universe of human LGBTQI, male and female homosexuality have received the most attention—and particularly male. However, bisexuality, transgender, queer/questioning and

[2] J. Balthazart, *The Biology of Homosexuality* (New York: Oxford University Press, 2012).

intersex are no less important, and perhaps no less prevalent. Scientific understanding of them lags behind homosexuality, but it will gradually catch up.

- Two levels of biology can contribute to sexual orientation and gender identity: genetics (DNA), and epigenetics. Either can exert an influence without the other, but generally one's sexuality is defined by the interaction of both.

- Sexual orientation and gender identity are "imprinted" during fetal development and are permanent. In other words, you are "born that way," whether gay or straight. (The notable exception to this statement appears to be in adult women, where sexual fluidity becomes more prevalent with age.) No amount of self-help or therapy can permanently alter the biological imprint.

Science matters. If we embrace the findings of science that sexual orientation and gender identity are biologically and indelibly imprinted during fetal development, and that they are varieties of normal, then we become a more just society and Church—as well as recipients of the enormous gifts that LGBTQI people bring to the table. But if we reject the findings of science and insist that homosexuality is just a bad choice that can be un-chosen, all of society—including the Church—suffers.

Choosing to Be "That Way"

This is John speaking. One of the primary differences many people see between LGBTQI people and the other oppressed groups discussed in previous chapters is the perceived element of choice. There is a perception among conservatives that LGBTQI people choose their sexual identity. I often hear conservatives say things like, "I do not condone that life-style choice." Or, "I don't see why she decided to go and be gay." The suggestion is that gay people have a choice about being gay, and that somehow, just to flout convention and be special, LGBTQI people simply decided to be "that way." I suspect that many people have cherished the notion of choice. Straight people are comfortable with the idea of choice because many don't understand why LGBTQI can't just choose to do the "right thing" and be straight. Some gay people have cherished this notion as well, hoping that they can-though God's grace and a lot of willpower- become straight. Now we understand why so many LGBTQI people say they have no experience of choice in the matter; it is because sexual orientation and gender identity are biologically and indelibly imprinted during fetal development. And yet, it takes many gay people a while to figure out that choice is more like wishful thinking than reality. With the Church and other major religions insisting everyone can choose their sexual orientation if only they love God enough, it can be extremely confusing. One hears from the pulpit that one has choice, and sometimes we hear testimonies from people (who are by definition bi-sexual) that they have become straight. So gay people may struggle to exercise that same framework of choice and find it doesn't work because they are gay, not bi. It is hard not to become self-condemning for failure to follow through on the "right" choice, and it is hard not to become depressed when one feels unable to control something so important which the Church says should, and must, be controlled.

Before the days when gay marriage was legal, "Rick and Steve" were a family in the progressive congregation I served. They volunteered in prominent roles, hosted church parties and socials in their home, and had their photo taken together for the church directory. They were filled with the Holy Spirit, and we had in common our love for Jesus Christ. Accepted, supported, and loved by the congregation, they were great guys, and I enjoyed their fellowship. They seemed completely comfortable with who they were individually and as a family.

After church one Sunday, Rick spoke to me briefly to say how much he had enjoyed worship. I had baptized the infant son of a much-loved family that morning, and the service had been especially beautiful. Rick went on to say that during the baptism, he prayed earnestly for the child. I thought that was a particularly appropriate and generous way to enter into the congregation's role in baptism, and commended him. Then he broke down emotionally. He said, "I always pray for the children who are baptized in our church. I pray that they will be straight, because being gay is so hard. No one wants to be gay, and no one choses to be gay. I would not wish it on anyone. It is so hard."

Rick was speaking for himself, describing his personal experience. Although his experience is not to be universalized, there is a lot of data that points to the difficulty of living LGBTQI in a straight world. If it were as simple as making a choice, many LGBTQI people would prefer to be straight. This is partly because gender norming is extremely powerful in society, and deviations are constantly targeted and punished, sometimes subtly and indirectly, and sometimes quite directly and brutally. There are many studies on the ways that LGBTQI people are punished for who they are. Most people would not choose such a difficult path just for the satisfaction of being different.

Rick and Steve were fortunate. They knew Jesus Christ in a personal way, and had a strong and vibrant faith. They had a stable, loving, and monogamous relationship with each other. They were accepted and supported as a family in the church. They were respected in the community. Even so, the stigma and social opprobrium of being gay was a heavy weight for them. I am just grateful that ours was the kind of church where gay people were particularly supported because the leaders in that church understood that extra grace, extra love, and extra support were needed to counterbalance the difficulty of being a misunderstood minority in a straight world.

A More Just Society and Loving Church

Until very recently, no one understood why some people are LGBTQI. Because of ignorance, it was attributed to weak or twisted morals. No one knew any better, although many loving Christians have always had a sense that extra grace was needed in these cases. This may also be the reason the scriptures do not really address quiet homosexuals living in committed and loving relationships. They were not understood very well, but somehow it was sensed that it was better to just apply a little grace and leave it alone. Now we understand exactly why this extra grace is needed. Each flavor of sexual orientation and identity on the LGBTQI spectrum is a tiny minority in comparison with the "straight" world. At best, it can be difficult and

The Church should be the preeminent place where LGBTQI people can find love, grace, support, acceptance, encouragement, and celebration of who God has created them to be.

lonely to be different from the larger society in such an important and defining way; at worst one can internalize the rejection and hate talk and wonder whether life is worth living.

The Church should be the preeminent place where LGBTQI people can find love, grace, support, acceptance, encouragement, and celebration of who God has created them to be. No less than the rest of us, LGBTQI people are "fearfully and wonderfully made" in the image of God. Instead, in many places, the Church is the last place where this kind of loving community is found.

Far from creating a safe, supportive and loving community for LGBTQI people, the Church has sometimes targeted them, ostracized them, treated them with contempt, and told them that they are an abomination to God worthy only to stoke the fires of hell. It hurts me to say that, and I imagine that it hurts you to read it. It is shameful, and astonishing, that people as loving and kind as we are have so persecuted LGBTQI people due to simple ignorance. The truth is, we thought they could change and that for their own good they *should* change. We thought LGBTQI orientation was just a sinful choice which could and should be repented. We thought we were acting in love to warn them about their sinfulness, to tell them the good news that their homosexuality was just a lie they had believed. We thought we were bringing good news that, by God's grace, God had created them straight if they would only repent and believe. We did not know how profoundly wrong we were; God had actually created them in a beautiful rainbow of colors we could not see. These unfortunate assumptions underlie the handful of scriptures that deal with homosexuality. Let's look at those scriptures in the next chapter.

A Christian whom I admire greatly and love as a brother in the Lord recently told me that genetics is no excuse for homosexuality. As I recall, he said that according to scripture, homosexuality is an immoral, evil, vile, disgraceful, shameful, ungodly, disgusting choice, and that those who practice it cannot enter the kingdom of God.

I share this with you for three reasons. First, my brother and good friend in the Lord has an opposite view on this than I. He is still my brother and good friend, and we will probably have opposite views until the Lord returns. I think it is good for us to "keep the unity of the Spirit in the bond of peace" (Eph. 4:3) even though our views diverge widely on this subject.

Second, I tell you this because a lot of conservatives say they love the sinner and hate the sin. If someone described you this way, would you believe they loved you? I am really sure I would not, and I would stay as far away from them as possible.

Third, my friend feels this way because he believes the Bible told him to believe this way. I think he is reading his Bible wrong. In our interpretation of the Bible, love always comes first; it trumps everything else. What he says about LGBTQI people is not any kind of love I can recognize. Rather, it conforms to definitions of abuse. In the next two chapters, we will see what the Bible actually says.

Questions for Reflection and Discussion

1. What does LGBTQI mean?

2. What evidence is there for genetic and epigenetic factors in sexual orientation and identity?

3. The Church has a love-hate relationship with science. It usually takes us a long time to accept scientific research that runs counter to our traditional interpretation of scripture. Where do you stand in accepting the science on genetics and sexuality?

4. The author said that the Church is preeminently a place where LGBTQI people should feel at home. What do you think?

5. When it comes to sexual orientation, is it possible to hate the "sin" without also hating the "sinner?"

For Further Research: Do a brief internet search on epigenetics. Try to make sure the people whose work you are reading are scientists.

6

What Does the Old Testament Say?

Before We Begin

Based on what I shared with you in the last chapter, I was prepared to simply "set aside" the scripture and tradition dealing with homosexuality. I thought I knew what the Old Testament had to say on that topic. Often enough, I had read the passages in Leviticus in my English translations. However, as I researched those passages for this book I took the trouble to read them in Hebrew, and to study them carefully in the context of the Old Testament as a whole and also in relation to the writings of St. Paul. I realized these passages were not nearly as simple as the English translations

These passages are not nearly as simple as the English translations make them appear.

make them appear.

The twentieth century has been somewhat obsessed with the idea of homosexuality as a very grave sin. The Church has traditionally supported this view. Can you imagine what would happen if Bible editors and publishers were to change the translations they sell to reflect recent scholarship suggesting that these scriptural passages actually forbid, not homosexuality in general, but specific sexual behaviors such as pederasty (men having sex with boys) and temple prostitution? There would be a terrible hue and cry, and those Bibles would sell very few copies. And yet, because more and more Bible scholars are aware of this context, better translations will eventually be published.

It is not my intention to try to make it seem that the Bible has nothing to say about homosexuality. However, all or most of the references to homosexuality in scripture address gang rape, pederasty, and ritualized temple prostitution. Most of us would make a distinction between these criminal behaviors and homosexual couples living in loving and committed relationships. It is uncertain how the authors of the Bible felt about quiet, committed homosexual relationships, because it seems to many that scripture simply does not discuss this. The Bible has been largely misunderstood on this subject, and we want to know exactly what the scriptures say in their context. However, progressives and many conservatives are also of the opinion that even if some scriptures condemn homosexual relationships, it is time to set aside those culture bound ideas, just as we moved beyond slavery and the oppression of women on the basis of compassionate, holy love. This is certainly my view. Nevertheless, reading and understanding scripture is a sacred thing. The scriptures we will examine in these two chapters can be interpreted in such a way as to condemn homosexual behavior, and I respect the Christian integrity of conservatives who read them that way. More legitimately and more accurately in my opinion, they condemn not homosexuality but the criminal behaviors we will examine below.

Less Than You Might Expect

As we saw in the last chapter, homosexuality is a steady factor in the natural world of over 1,500 species, including humans. Scientists believe the percentage of LGBTQI people has held steady over time at around 2.5-5%. So it should not surprise us that homosexuality is mentioned in both the Old and New Testaments, because it was certainly a known factor in the ancient world. What might surprise us is that as prevalent as homosexuality was in ancient times- roughly as prevalent as today- simple homosexuality is seldom, if ever, mentioned in the Bible. When homosexual behavior is mentioned, the concern seems connected with behaviors that are still crimes in the United States like rape, pedaphilia, and prostitution. Other than this, homosexual behavior simply was not of great concern in the ancient world, either in the Old or New Testament periods. There are only six scripture passages that deal directly with homosexuality, and we will look at them together. We will also look briefly at all the passages that mention "sodomites."

It is interesting that, when it comes to homosexuality, conservative Christians are vitally interested in what the Bible has to say. We are truly sincere about this, although many are far less interested in what the Bible has to say about tithing or the treatment of immigrants, even though scripture has a great deal to say about the latter in multiple passages that are unambiguous and strongly worded. That is, on certain subjects the least utterance of scripture seems eternally binding for conservatives, but on other subjects such as immigration, scripture seems all but irrelevant. Conservatives accuse progressives of cherry picking only the scriptures they like, but seem to have little self-awareness that they themselves disregard great portions of the Bible while waving other passages like a tattered battle flag. The truth is that all Christians seek to hear what scripture says, but different passages resonate more deeply with different people. We all know instinctively that scripture is written in a certain cultural context that must be understood, translated and filtered. Conservatives pretend we don't filter, but we do. We should probably give up that pretense; it is dishonest and makes us look like we lack self-awareness.

Many conservative Christians are so repulsed by homosexuality, and in some ways are so afraid that it is a contagious choice- "Will our children become gay if they hang out with gay people? Will our children become gay if we act like it is perfectly okay and don't stigmatize it?"- that these scriptures sometimes seem more important than anything else the Bible has to say. Probably one of the reasons for this is that we know LGTBQI people are treated badly, and we do not wish that for anyone, especially our children. But we now know that LGBTQI persons are born that way; it isn't caught or taught. So perhaps the solution is to stop treating LGBTQI as "less than," and to begin to follow the command of Jesus to love them as we ourselves would wish to be loved.

Some conservative Christians are sufficiently angry about this issue to leave their denomination, and to call those who remain, "apostate." It would be more appropriate for Christians to firmly reject notions that cause LGBTQI people to be mistreated. It would also be appropriate to meditate on the numerous scriptures that teach the virtue of patient, tolerant unity in the Church. But unity when important principles are at stake requires spiritual maturity. It is much easier to take one's marbles and go home.

Since homosexuality is one of the white-hot social issues of our day, it is difficult for us to realize that this was simply not the case in biblical times. If homosexuality were a more important issue the biblical writers would have discussed it more often and more thoroughly in scripture. Love, mercy, justice, faith, stewardship, and prayer are discussed over and over in scripture. But homosexuality is mentioned in only approximately six passages. . . because it is just not that important. Someone might suggest that it was not mentioned because everyone "knew better anyway." Even a cursory review of sexuality in the ancient Near East will reveal that this was not the case in either the Old or New Testament context.

Those Six Scriptures Are Hard To Translate

When we read our Bibles in English, it is not difficult to understand what they say, especially with the more modern translations. This is because translators have worked with the Greek and Hebrew texts to give us a smooth and clear interpretation. When I began to research those six scriptures in the Hebrew and Greek, I was surprised to learn that their meaning is far from clear. This is uncomfortable for us. We want our English translations to be rock solid, and in most respects they are. But ancient Hebrew and Greek are languages where translators sometimes have to fill in the blanks, and the words or phrases that come before and after modify the meanings without specific connectors. Sometimes the way we connect those words and fill in the blanks can change the meaning from one shade to another. This is especially evident in the Corinthian and Timothy texts, because how one word modifies another in the "list of sins" can change the meaning of the phrase, as we will see in the next chapter. So whereas English is usually quite clear in the way one word functions to modify another word in a sentence or phrase, Greek and Hebrew sometimes are not as clear.

One of the safeguards for interpreting scripture is that when we find a passage in Hebrew or Greek that is unclear, we can refer to other places in the Bible that use the same words and phrases. From the context of those other usages, we can shed light on the words or phrases we are examining.

This is an extremely reliable method in most questions of Biblical teaching, but it isn't very helpful with the question at hand. Because homosexuality is not seen as a major problem in biblical times, it is seldom mentioned. Since it is seldom mentioned, we do not have many opportunities to compare one verse with another for meaning; however, when we do compare those six passages idol worship, cult prostitution, pederasty, or gang rape are always in the context. So if we are using one passage to illuminate another, the six passages all have in common this kind of abuse.

In looking carefully at the scriptures that deal with homosexuality, and the ways they have been translated over the centuries, we see that the homosexual problems addressed in scripture are more complicated than we thought. Simply put,

There is a modern desire to reduce the complexity to a simple, blanket prohibition ...

these six scriptures are not straightforward. They are fraught with difficulty because homosexuality in the ancient world was complex, but when the scriptures relating to homosexuality are translated, there is a modern desire to reduce the complexity to a simple, blanket prohibition of any homosexual behavior. That may be well intentioned, but it is not honest. For example, when a text says that pederasty is prohibited, how is that to be translated? Are we to translate it to say that pederasty is forbidden, or should it say that homosexuality is forbidden?

Either translation communicates the condemnation of pederasty, but the latter carries an additional condemnation that is not called for. Another example is that in the original Hebrew, all the passages in the Old Testament that mention anything connected with homosexual practice use exclusively male nouns. They do not use both male and female nouns for the behavior they seek to abolish, whatever behavior that is. But some translations such as the Living Bible or the NLT render this as "*homosexuality* is...a detestable sin." That way, they can mistranslate the text and make it seem to apply to lesbians as well as gays. But the Hebrew clearly does not include women in the scriptural references. Many biblical scholars believe this is because pederasty, and not homosexuality, is being addressed. But in any case, women are not addressed in any text relating to homosexual practice, with the possible exception of Romans, which addresses pederasty and cult prostitution on a dramatic scale. All the other texts clearly and exclusively refer to males. So where is all that Bible teaching on lesbians?

A moment ago, I was talking about the usefulness of comparing one passage with another to understand meaning. Most or all of the references to homosexuality in the Bible have rape, prostitution, pedaphilia or the sexualized worship of fertility gods as the context. Does the writer intend to forbid all homosexual relationships, or is the writer addressing specific kinds of sexual relationships like homosexual prostitution and pederasty? Forbidding either of these is very different from forbidding all homosexual relationships. In general, it has been encouraged for translators to make a broader translation than the texts have called for, because the Church agreed that homosexuality in all its forms was simply wrong. But once this assumption was called into question, and the texts were examined more critically, scholars began to see that the texts may have been interpreted too broadly. These translations are now in flux. If you look at your Bible at home, you will probably see a broad translation for the texts we will explore here. But increasingly, biblical scholars are calling these translations into question and future translations will reflect the more narrow, and more accurate renderings. We conservatives do not usually welcome the idea that our English translations need to be adjusted because of more intensive research into the original languages, but we deserve to know that this is in process, and it is legitimate. Let's dive in.

Power Differentials and Fertility Gods

There are basically four kinds of homosexual behavior addressed in the Bible: rape as a demonstration of turf and dominance, men taking advantage of male slaves and weaker men, fertility god worship with temple prostitution, and pederasty; often the last three were combined. A way to look at this is to check references to the word, "sodomy" in various ancient translations of the Bible. References to any form of non-procreative sex (heterosexual, homosexual, or with animals) was viewed as sodomy. Indeed, the Roman Catholic Church has maintained to this day that any sex act that is not procreative or open to procreation is wrong. Although most Christians no longer have this view, recall that this was the theological impetus behind the old English and colonial sodomy laws. Today, we practice birth control and many engage in sodomy with spouses. It is important to note that sodomy was not concerned simply with homosexuality; it was concerned with any form of non-procreative sex.

That condemns most heterosexual couples as well as homosexual couples.

The search for references to sodomy in scripture will pull up references to Genesis 19:5-8 (homosexual gang rape), Exodus 22:19 (bestiality, not homosexuality), Leviticus 18:22-23 (homosexuality and bestiality) and 20:13-15 (homosexuality and bestiality), Deuteronomy 23:17 (cult prostitutes) and 27:21 (bestiality), Judges 19:22 (homosexual gang rape), I Kings 14:24 (cult prostitutes), 15:12 (cult prostitutes), 22:46 (cult prostitutes), II Kings 23:7 (cult prostitutes), Romans 1:24-27 (fertility cult worship), I Corinthians 6:9 (pederasty and prostitution), and I Timothy 1:9-10 (pederasty and prostitution). Two of the references are to male gang rape, and two refer exclusively to bestiality, not to heterosexuality or homosexuality. The Leviticus texts may refer exclusively to homosexuality, but many scholars see them as referring to pederasty and cult prostitution. The other texts all involve some connection with prostitution or pederasty. The overwhelming concern of biblical references to homosexuality have to do with gang rape, pederasty, and cult prostitution. If we follow the method of allowing differing passages to help interpret others, we see the common link with behaviors which are unquestionably outlawed in the United States today. These passages are not about LGBTQI people who want to live faithfully in a committed relationship. Let's look closer at some of the behaviors.

Homosexual behavior in the Old and New Testament periods is exclusively written about from the perspective of heterosexual men. Across time and cultures, the vast majority of men are heterosexual. Since passive homosexual men who were penetrated like women were pitied and scorned, homosexuals were not in a position to form and express scriptural notions, or to form public opinion on the subject. LGBTQI voices were simply not heard. The primary concern of heterosexual men concerning homosexual behavior was the idea of a man being raped or used like a woman by more powerful men. In the ancient world, this was something to be endured by less powerful males. As stronger men used the weaker either for gratification or violent humiliation, or both, scriptural teachings on the subject were intended to protect weaker heterosexual men from the more powerful, much like the sodomy laws we discussed in Chapter 1. For example, in ancient times, victorious invading armies raped not only women but also enemy soldiers they had conquered. And remember, everyone was assumed to be heterosexual deep down; those who behaved differently were seen as pitifully confused.

There were also temple or cult prostitutes in Israel associated with the worship of fertility gods. Temple prostitutes in Northern Israel were both male and female, and were not simply free people earning a living, (although cult prostitution in some ancient cultures was at times more voluntary and socially acceptable). These prostitutes, both male and female, had to endure the penetration of those who were socially and economically more powerful. Scriptural prohibitions against men having sex with men were designed to offer a religious foundation of protection for physically, economically, socially, and militarily weaker men. As we look at these scriptures together, we will see the kindness and justice of scripture which was meant to protect less powerful heterosexual men from sexual abuse. These scriptures are also intended to prohibit participation in the worship of the Canaanite fertility cults, which included male and female temple prostitutes. Written exclusively from a heterosexual viewpoint, these scriptures do not address the needs or experiences of LGBTQI people. Since homosexual activity was subsumed by these abusive power differentials, the needs and concerns of LGBTQI people who simply wanted to live in a loving, committed relationship were not of interest and were not addressed.

Rather, scripture addressed Israel's appropriate anxiety concerning the fertility cults and the abuse of men by more powerful heterosexual males. Perhaps the textbook case for this is the story of Sodom and Gomorrah.

Genesis 18-19 Sodom and Gomorrah

In Genesis 18 and 19 we see the extreme contrast between the way the righteous and the unrighteous treat strangers. In Genesis 18, the scene is rural. Abraham is a wealthy man, primarily nomadic. Three men, whom Abraham apparently does not recognize as angels, come to Abraham. As soon as he sees them, he bows to them and entreats them to accept his hospitality. He offers them water and rest under his shade tree while a luxurious meal of bread, cream and fresh veal is prepared for them. They are treated with utmost care, honor, and hospitality. God offers Abraham his blessing through them.

Then God shares with Abraham his intention of destroying the cities of Sodom and Gomorrah, because of their great wickedness. Two of the angels then go to Sodom. They appear as ordinary men. When they arrive in the city, Abraham's nephew, Lot, sees them and invites them to his home. Again, we see the connection between righteousness, hospitality, and caring for the stranger. Lot is righteous and offers hospitality to the vulnerable stranger. The angels insist that they will spend the night in the public square, but Lot eventually prevails and they come home with him to enjoy his hospitality. It is to be surmised that the angels wanted to spend the night in the square in order to get a better idea of the moral disposition of the populace. But no matter, because the men of Sodom were so evil, they came to seek out Lot's two guests. All the men of the city surrounded Lot's house and demanded that he surrender to them the two strangers he was hosting, for the purposes of gang rape with death as a probable result. The angels struck the men blind. God gave Lot and his family time to evacuate, and then God destroyed the city with fire.

We see a very similar episode in Judges 19, contrasting the way the righteous and the unrighteous treat strangers. A Levite and his concubine were traveling from Bethlehem to Ephraim. They stopped in Gibeah for the night, thinking that since they were among fellow Israelites, they would be safe. An old man invited them to spend the night in his home. He was righteous, offering hospitality to vulnerable strangers. Suddenly some men from the town surrounded the house and demanded the surrender of the Levite so they could gang rape and then kill him. Instead, the concubine was surrendered. She was raped all night and died before dawn. The rest of the tribes of Israel were outraged by this, and they united to destroy Gibeah completely.

Gang rape of men in the ancient world was not as unusual as we would like to think. The functions of these two stories in the Old Testament are the same: to let it be known that abuse and gang rape of strangers is a serious

The behavior on trial is the abuse of marginalized persons. . .

crime against God and society, and is punishable by death to the entire city that harbors these criminals. Once again, we do not have an instance of Adam and Steve falling in love and quietly living together. That is not mentioned, and that is not the behavior that is on trial. The behavior on trial is the abuse of marginalized persons, including the gang rape and murder of vulnerable strangers, as a demonstration of turf and dominance. Jude 1:7 mentions the immorality of Sodom and Gomorrah but is unclear about the nature of the immorality. In the Greek it says literally that they went after "strange flesh." Is this a reference to trying to gang-rape strangers, or is this a reference to trying to gang-rape angels? It is hard to tell. Other internal scriptural references to Sodom consistently interpret the sin of Sodom as failing to care for vulnerable people. For example, see Isaiah 1:10-17 and Ezekial 16:49-50. Is it possible that the sin of Sodom actually convicts us conservatives when we fail to care for vulnerable LGBTQI people?

Leviticus 18:21-23 (NRSV) *You shall not give any of your offspring to sacrifice them to Molech, and so profane the name of your God: I am the Lord. You shall not lie with a male as with a woman; it is an abomination. You shall not have sexual relations with any animal and defile yourself with it, nor shall any woman give herself to an animal to have sexual relations with it: it is perversion.*
Leviticus 20:13 (NRSV) *If a man lies with a male as with a woman, both of them have committed an abomination; they shall be put to death; their blood is upon them.*

We will deal with these two passages together, because they exist in the same context and have essentially the same message. The setting for Leviticus is that the Israelite slaves have escaped from Egypt, and they are traveling toward Canaan, the Promised Land. They have not yet become a nation; they are a huge group of rag-tag escaped slaves wandering through the dessert. They have few laws, institutions, religious traditions, and no country of their own. Culturally, they are as close to zero as they can get. God is starting from scratch forming them into a nation with a distinct religion, culture, country, and institutions. This is not onerous to God. God has chosen to make these people who were no people, his people.

These laws were given to a people on the move, at the beginning of their journey of civilization. The prohibition against men raping weaker men was a step in the direction of justice, in a world where male on male rape was a means to demonstrate dominance and define turf. These laws protected weaker men from stronger, vicious men. No one wants to turn back that clock. Rape should be a criminal act no matter the victim. But this law was also a blunt instrument. It protected weaker men from rape and abuse, but the spill-over effect was that it also affected LGBTQI people who simply wanted a loving and committed same sex relationship.

Additionally, there was a tremendous concern with cult prostitution. One of the great challenges for the Hebrew people as they entered Canaan was the dominance of the fertility gods and goddesses. Throughout the Old Testament, there was a constant concern about whether the Israelites would be faithful to God or whether they would prostitute themselves by worshipping the fertility gods. In fact, you may have noticed that the texts in Isaiah 1 and Ezekial 16 mentioned above deal with the worship of fertility gods. The fertility gods were worshipped in ritualized sexual practices including orgies with both male and female prostitutes. The Old Testament writers were very much concerned with the worship of the fertility gods, because this was a violation of the first and most important commandment to worship only *Yawheh*, the God of Israel. We will see that this concern did not abate in the New Testament period. Notice that in Leviticus, the prohibition against male on male sex comes in the same line with a prohibition against worshipping the fertility god, Molech. Some people read this text as prohibiting the worship of the fertility god Molech by giving him one's sperm through intercourse with male or female cult prostitutes or by engaging in the bestiality which was also part of the worship of fertility gods. In Leviticus 18:21, the word translated as offspring or seed in many English translations is literally translated in the Septuagint as sperm (*spermatos*). Others see a connection between Leviticus 20:13 and the male cult prostitutes referred to in the books of First and Second Kings and Deuteronomy.

There are additional reasons to view the Leviticus passages as dealing with cult prostitution and pederasty. As we will see in the next chapter, in Romans 1, Paul is dealing with temple prostitution, pederasty, and worship of the female fertility gods.

Martin Luther also viewed the Leviticus passages as addressing pederasty.

In Romans 1:32 he says, "God's decree says that people who do such things deserve death." This is a clear reference to Leviticus 20:13, and by "such things" Paul indicates that his interpretation of Leviticus is that it deals with the same problem he himself addresses: temple prostitution and pederasty. In addition, see the section on Corinthians and Timothy in Chapter 7. Here, we reference a contemporary of Paul's named Philo, a Jewish historian and theologian who writes a commentary on Leviticus. He also interprets Leviticus as addressing pederasty and cult prostitution, describing a situation very similar to the one described by Paul in Romans 1.

Martin Luther also viewed the Leviticus passages as addressing pederasty. Luther translated the word rendered "male" in the above translations as "boy" in each of the Leviticus passages cited above. Martin Luther translated it as *Du sollst nicht bei Knaben liegen wie beim Weibe; denn es ist ein*

Greuel, which is 'You shall not lie with a boy as with a woman; for it is an abomination.' So when progressives say that Leviticus refers to pederasty and cult prostitution, this is an understanding that reaches back to the first century and is reflected in the sixteenth century scholarship of Martin Luther; it is not an idea recently seized upon by progressives. I will not suggest that "boy" is the only possible way to translate these passages in Leviticus, but it is an appropriate way. Again, the concern was not about Adam and Steve, it was about pederasty and cult prostitution.

Who is Going to 'Walk Back' Leviticus 20:13?

A conservative friend recently said to me, "Somebody's going to have to 'walk back' Leviticus 20:13 before I can agree that homosexuality is not a sin." I think my friend is going to have to walk back Leviticus 20:13 for himself, because he is not a murderer. Let me explain.

If you look at Leviticus 20:13, and translate it as "male" instead of "boy," do you believe this is literally the binding commandment of God, not to be broken? Think carefully before you answer, because nearly everyone would say that they certainly do not advocate execution for homosexuals, and yet that is exactly what Leviticus

20:13b commands. If you are conservative, and if you take Leviticus 20:13a literally, please explain exactly how you can disregard 20:13b? You certainly would not say it is because we don't live in a theocracy and the Church hasn't the authority to call for capital punishment, because even if you did have authority to impose capital punishment in this case, you would not do it. Why can't I legitimately reject Leviticus 20:13a if you can legitimately reject Leviticus 20:13b? Please think about that. It is important. Because what it demonstrates is that both conservatives and progressives reject scriptures that are unloving and culture bound. Conservatives are right in perceiving that Leviticus 20:13b is culture bound. Progressives are right in perceiving that, when interpreted as addressing homosexuality in general rather than pederasty, Leviticus20:13 is culture bound in its entirety. Who is cherry picking? Ahhh hmm. Both. That is because the entire passage is culture bound.

Have You Committed An Abomination Today?

The first five books of the Old Testament, also called the Pentateuch, detail the beginnings of Israel. Leviticus is one of those books. As we read the Pentateuch, we see the marvelous way that God quickly begins to give them an identity with their own laws, customs and religious rituals. Some of their laws are very similar to those of other ancient Near Eastern nations. Some are purposefully quite distinct. It is the laws that are distinct that interest us here, because that is where the root of the word, "abomination" comes from. The word translated as "abomination" or "detestable act" depending on the translation, means "ritually unclean." Having sex with relatives, men having sex with cult prostitutes, eating foods such as pork or shellfish, sacrificing children, oppressing one's neighbor, and having sex with one's wife during her period, are all abominations. Today, we would not regard these behaviors as being morally equivalent, but they are all abominations for God's people at that time.

Other books of the Bible lengthen the list of abominations to include lending money at interest, having a proud look, lying, and gossiping. There are many things which the Bible says are an abomination, but which seem perfectly fine to us, such as loaning money at interest, and eating shrimp, lobster, or bacon. On the other hand, some of these things seem deeply and disturbingly wicked, like incest and child sacrifice. What this means is that "abomination" in and of itself is not much of a guide for us today in terms of moral right and wrong.

So is it an abomination to have bacon and eggs for breakfast, eat a ham sandwich for lunch, surf and turf for dinner, and then to round out a great day by making love to one's wife even if it hasn't been seven days since her period? Most of us don't think so, but Leviticus tells us these are all abominations. Can you imagine going to your bank and telling everyone who works there that they are an abomination because it was an abomination for the Israelites to lend money at interest to other Israelites? The concern here is that a few Christians use the word abomination like a club to beat LGBTQI people. That needs to stop because it is both hateful and inaccurate. Before we say that homosexuality is an "abomination" we should take a look at our own way of living, because according to that same Levitical standard, most of us are also practicing "abominations".

Male on Male Sex

What about male on male sex? We cannot know with certainty the full intention of the biblical authors. But we do know that much of what was forbidden by Israel's laws is still repugnant to all of us. Men raping men to express turf and dominance is deeply disturbing. Men taking advantage of boys, slaves, or cult and temple prostitutes is disgusting. These highly abusive practices are the primary expressions of male homosexuality addressed by scripture in ancient Israel; and not the simple love and commitment between two people of the same sex.

Deuteronomy 23:17 says, "none of the sons of Israel shall be a temple prostitute." The book of Deuteronomy is contemporaneous with Leviticus, and in some ways Deuteronomy is a summing up of the laws given in Leviticus, putting them in theological context for the community. Male temple prostitution was enough of a problem that it had to be addressed officially, and it may well be that the context for this proscription given in Deuteronomy explains the context and application of the law given in Leviticus. That is not a case of simple LGBTQI orientation and identity. Some translators have seen a clear linguistic connection between the Leviticus passages we are discussing and temple prostitution, which included pederasty. That is, a reasonable translation of the passages is that they forbid pederasty and male temple prostitution. It is doubtful that the small percentage of the population who were LGBTQI would have aroused enough visibility to require the formation of laws; however, the lewd nature of cult prostitution which was attached to the worship of fertility gods was widespread in the ancient Near East and was a potent challenge to faith in the God of Israel. This kind of threat would require the formation of laws.

We must also consider how men were viewed in ancient culture. In many ancient cultures, including Israel, being a man was considered a holy thing. The human male was the apotheosis of creation. Men were of infinitely higher rank, stature, and value than women. Judaism is the religion which for the past two thousand years assiduously taught Jewish men to pray every morning: "Blessed are you, Lord, our God, ruler of the universe who has not created me a woman." In the hierarchy of the world, men were at the top. Women were owned by men.

For a man to have sex with another man as with a woman was to demean the receiver, to debase a man to the shameful role of a woman. If the dominant male debased another man in this way, this was seen as a terrible crime and injustice. If a man debased himself by consenting to be put in the feminine role, this was a crime against himself. The thought was that he should understand his privileged role as a man and glory in it. Under no circumstances should he surrender the glory of the masculine.

It is degrading for LGBTQI to pretend to be straight

Haven't we outgrown this male-centric worldview?
Do we really believe that women are so far beneath
men, so pathetically low, that a man degrades
himself when he takes the receptive role in sex?
Today, Christians believe in the equal humanity
and dignity of both women and men, but ancient
Near Eastern societies certainly did not view the
world in that way. We have mentioned that there is
no Old Testament prohibition against women
having sex with women. Many biblical scholars
suggest that this is because, since they are already
women, they cannot degrade themselves further
by coupling. I think we have outgrown all that.

Some conservatives might suggest that the concern
today is not that women are lower than men, but
that it is degrading when people do what is
unnatural, that is, when people behave contrary to
the roles for which they were created by God. But
if LGBTQI people were created by God that way in
the womb, then when they follow their LGBTQI
orientation and identity they are indeed doing
what is natural for them, and they are behaving in
the way God intended. What is extremely
degrading for LGBTQI persons is to pretend to be
something God did not create them to be.

Questions for Reflection and Discussion

1. Are you surprised that so few scriptures directly address homosexuality? Why do you think it is seldom addressed?

2. Why do you suppose lesbianism is not mentioned in the Old Testament?

3. If scripture was written by heterosexual men, would this have had an impact on the scriptural view of homosexuality? Why or why not? To what degree do the perspectives and personalities of the writers shine through in shaping scripture?

4. What is the crime of Sodom? Do other passages in the Bible shed light on this view?

5. Describe the primary contexts for homosexual behavior as described in the Old Testament. Do you see references to two people seeking to love one another in a committed relationship, or do these passages seem concerned about other matters such as cult prostitution, pederasty and rape?

For Further Research: Do an internet search on "shrine prostitution."

7

What Does the New Testament Say?

As I mentioned in the previous chapter, I had decided to simply set aside the culture bound scripture and tradition referring to homosexuality. However, when I began the research for this book, I was stunned to discover that the New Testament passages which are translated in reference to homosexuality seem more accurately to refer to pederasty and temple prostitution.

Homosexuality in the Roman World

The New Testament was written in a world dominated by Rome. In the Roman world, power over others included both opportunity and permission for sexual abuse. As discussed earlier, slavery was an integral part of ancient societies. Slaves were at the mercy of their masters, and were not at liberty to reject their sexual advances. Slave owners might commonly and without moral disapproval require sexual gratification from women or from youths they possessed, male or female. Jews objected to using male slaves in this way. Nevertheless, in the Roman world beautiful boys were particularly highly prized as sexual objects. When these slave boys were castrated to preserve their appeal, they were called catamites. This practice was reserved primarily for the rich and powerful who were so inclined.

Sexual abuse was not limited to the slave relationship, but could be a factor in many types of relationships where there was a power differential, even among the upper classes. For example, the Roman emperor Caligula (12-41 A.D.) subjected both high ranking male officials and their wives to his voracious sexual appetites and made a public display of the same at banquets by requiring his guests to have sex with him. The details given by Suetonius in *The Lives of the Caesars* are lascivious. He embodied every possible kind of cruelty and evil, demanded to be worshipped as a god and was assassinated by his officers. Suetonius records that some of his assassins shoved their swords through Caligula's private parts, no doubt because he had given them cause. Caligula's atrocities were infamous, and Paul seems to have had the still-reverberating details of his story in mind as he wrote Romans 1, especially the part about receiving in one's own person the due penalty for error. This formed part of a larger story of sexual abuse by the powerful, combined with pederasty and temple prostitution on an almost unimaginable scale.

Pederasty

Pederasty was a somewhat common practice in ancient Greek and Roman societies, and was another manifestation of the sexualization of power differentials. Pederasty was a sexual friendship between a man and a male youth. The morality of pederasty was sometimes debated in the ancient world, and in some centuries it was more accepted than in others. Some people thought pederasty was a positive moral good, others thought it was shameful, but according to the Sibylline oracles, Jews never accepted the practice. Since the youth involved was not yet a man, it was not universally regarded as shameful for him to be in the receptive sexual role. Nevertheless, once the youth had a beard, he had become a man and the friendship was no longer to be sexual.

Often, Pederasty was approved of and arranged by the parents. The relationship was thought to teach a youth how to become a man, and to establish strong bonds of love between a youth and an older man who could help the young man profitably make his way in life. This relationship apparently did not make the youths into homosexuals, and this would make sense since sexual orientation is fixed in the womb. We will talk about pederasty more in our discussion of I Corinthians and I Timothy.

Sexual relationships created by power differentials, such as pederasty, slavery, and temple prostitution, were common in the Roman world of

> *Homosexuality is not rejected by the scriptures, but rather rape, pederasty, and homosexual temple prostitution.*

Paul's day, and as a pious Jew and Christian, Paul was deeply disgusted. All of us would agree. The idea of anyone- male or female- being forced to submit to sex because of a power differential ignites our anger and indignation. Compound this with the revulsion most men have to the idea of being penetrated by another man, and we can more than understand Paul's objections to homosexuality as it was largely practiced in the ancient world. Any argument which could be made among people of faith to eschew such abuses would be a good and positive step. Yet, notice that all the passages in the New Testament are connected with temple prostitutes or pederasty. It is not homosexuality that is rejected by the scriptures, but rather rape, pederasty, and homosexual temple prostitution.

Romans 1:18-32 (NRSV)

18 For the wrath of God is revealed from heaven against all ungodliness and wickedness of those who by their wickedness suppress the truth. 19 For what can be known about God is plain to them, because God has shown it to them. 20 Ever since the creation of the world his eternal power and divine nature, invisible though they are, have been understood and seen through the things he has made. So they are without excuse; 21 for though they knew God, they did not honor him as God or give thanks to him, but they became futile in their thinking, and their senseless minds were darkened. 22 Claiming to be wise, they became fools; 23 and they exchanged the glory of the immortal God for images resembling a mortal human being or birds or four-footed animals or reptiles.

24 Therefore God gave them up in the lusts of their hearts to impurity, to the degrading of their bodies among themselves, 25 because they exchanged the truth about God for a lie and worshiped and served the creature rather than the Creator, who is blessed forever! Amen. 26 For this reason God gave them up to degrading passions. Their women exchanged natural intercourse for unnatural, 27 and in the same way also the men, giving up natural intercourse with women, were consumed with passion for one another. Men committed shameless acts with men and received in their own persons the due penalty for their error.

28 And since they did not see fit to acknowledge God, God gave them up to a debased mind and to things that should not be done. 29 They were filled with every kind of wickedness, evil, covetousness, malice. Full of envy, murder, strife, deceit, craftiness, they are gossips, 30 slanderers, God-haters, insolent, haughty, boastful, inventors of evil, rebellious toward parents, 31 foolish, faithless, heartless, ruthless. 32 They know God's decree, that those who practice such things deserve to die—yet they not only do them but even applaud others who practice them.

They No Longer Exist

As I made my journey from assuming homosexuality was a sin to realizing it is not, this passage had a gradual and increasingly profound impact on me. Of the six scanty scriptural references to homosexuality, all except this one are limited to just a few words. But this passage in Romans is very different. It comprises fourteen full verses, and gives a complete theological framework of the sin discussed there. It traces a fallen state of humanity from its origins in unrepentant idol worship, to its expression in violent orgies, to complete moral failure, and finally to God's rejection. Like many Christians, I used to assume Paul was speaking about LGBTQI people in Romans 1. Gradually, I realized this interpretation simply does not fit. Finally, I researched the cultural context and learned that the problem Paul was addressing no longer exists. Since this passage is viewed by conservatives as the most comprehensive treatment of homosexuality in the Bible, we will spend more time on this passage than the others. Let's explore this together.

Have you ever read this passage and thought there was something about it that just didn't fit? Maybe you have a son, daughter or close friend who identifies as LGBTQI. Does this passage match the people you know and love who are homosexual? Honestly, I do not know anyone who fits Paul's description, and I'll bet you don't either. Yes, we know plenty of men who are attracted to men, and women who are attracted to women. But a lot of those folks are certainly not idol worshippers. Many are faithful United Methodists, Episcopalians, Roman Catholics, and other Christians. These folks aren't idol worshippers, they worship the Lord Jesus Christ. And they are not filled with malice, they are filled with the Holy

Spirit. Obviously they are not murderers as the people referred to in this passage are; they love God and neighbor, just as fully and imperfectly as straight believers do. So why doesn't this biblical description match our real life experience? It is because this is not a description of LGBTQI people in general. Paul's passage refers to worshippers and priests of the fertility goddess cults which were popular throughout the Roman empire of his day. The reason you don't know any of these people is because, even though they were infamous in Paul's day, they no longer exist.

The Context: Female Fertility Cults

We now know clearly that Romans 1 is written in the context of the female fertility cults of the Roman world, making this a prime example of a culture bound text. Since it refers to a narrowly defined group of people who no longer exist, most of us do not understand who Paul is talking about. This is a good example of the need to understand the cultural situation of a passage in order to interpret it. Without scholarship and research, passages which are culture bound are invisible to us. If we knew they referred only to a specific problem in that culture, we would not misinterpret them. But since we don't realize it, we become the blind leading the blind. To say that Romans 1 condemns homosexuals is like saying that the story of Sodom and Gomorrah condemns men. The former is no more about homosexuals in general than the latter is about men in general.

Here is the tragic way this text is usually misinterpreted. People see verses 26 and 27, and they think that here, Paul is talking about homosexuals. So they assume that the entire passage, including verses 18-25 and verses 28-32 are also talking about ordinary homosexuals. Their conclusion from verses 18-25 is that, as a class, homosexuals are: 1) under the wrath of God, 2) wicked, 3) suppressors of the truth, 4) rejecters of God's revelation, 5) futile and senseless, with darkened minds, 6) fools, 7) idol worshippers, and 8) abandoned by God. In addition, from verses 28-32 many people believe that the Bible is teaching that all homosexuals are unutterably wicked and deserving of death: *filled with every kind of wickedness, evil, covetousness, malice. Full of envy, murder, strife, deceit, craftiness, they are gossips, slanderers, God-haters, insolent, haughty, boastful, inventors of evil, rebellious toward parents, foolish, faithless, heartless, ruthless. They know God's decree, that those who practice such things deserve to die—yet they not only do them but even applaud others who practice them.*

This is the indescribable opprobrium with which LGBTQI people have lived throughout the Christian era. With this passage interpreted in ignorance, all homosexuals are assumed to be evil; all are assumed to be deserving of death, spared only by some mysterious grace. Some Christian LGBTQI people, who cannot change their biologically determined sexual orientation or identity, have heard these words so many times that they have despaired of life utterly and taken their lives. They have believed that they are abandoned by God and worthy of death, because they mistakenly believe God's word says so, and many churches have reinforced this erroneous interpretation. Others are under psychiatric care as they try to silence in their minds these powerful words of scripture which have been completely and tragically misunderstood. The Church needs to put a stop to this dark and abusive misinterpretation. It isn't merely theology or theory. People are dying because of this, which is a sign that the theology is out of balance. If people had the ability to choose, as heterosexual conservatives imagine to be the case, they would do so. Since they are told they must change and cannot, many feel ultimate despair and utterly forsaken by God.

So whom did Paul have in mind as he wrote Romans 1? Paul felt intensely emotional as he wrote this. We know that Paul sometimes has emotional outbursts; that is one of the ways scholars identify his letters as authentically written by him. He was having one of those moments as he wrote Romans 1:18-32, and it was explosive. Why was Paul so angry?

As Paul wrote this section of Romans, he was referring to devotees and priests of certain religious cults which were well known in the Roman world and whose excesses were generally held in contempt by the population. The worship of the fertility goddesses was quite popular, but the excesses of the Galli described by Paul, and by others whom I will cite, were beyond the pale. Homosexuality was certainly known in the Roman world; in some ways it was accepted, and yet it was simultaneously frowned upon in some ways. Let's look closer.

Take pederasty, for example. For a grown man to be in the receptive role was regarded as shameful, and Rome was a culture fixated upon the dominating virility of the male citizen. As I have mentioned before, male prostitutes and male slaves were regarded as fair game, but no male citizen could undertake the passive role without shame. So I do not mean to suggest that the passive homosexual role for male citizens was regarded positively; it was not. Nor do I suggest that homosexual behavior was generally approved by Jewish tradition; Greeks and Romans were more lenient in this respect than Jews, and you will recall that Paul's religious heritage and training were eminently Jewish. But the damning language of Romans 1 is not directed toward normal, loving and committed homosexual relationships. Scriptural references in general, and Paul's letter to the Romans in specific, were directed toward the aggressive, sometimes violent and self-harming fertility cults, which were known to oppose Paul directly, and vice-versa.

In Romans 1, Paul is specifically referring to devotees and priests of certain religious fertility cults. These cults included the worship of Dionysus, Cybele (another name for

> *Paul's letter addressed the aggressive, violent and self-harming fertility cults,*

Aphrodite), Attis (Cybele's divine, self-castrated consort), and Artemis of the Ephesians. To say that Paul was not on friendly terms with these folks would be a gross understatement. You may recall that the Jews were mortal enemies of fertility cults as far back as the time of Moses, and the Old Testament references to sodomites we saw in the previous chapter referred to these fertility cult male prostitutes. Nothing was different for Paul on that score. Paul went from city to city in the ancient world bringing the good news of Jesus Christ. He aggressively taught the monotheism of Christianity and in good Jewish tradition he went head to head with the polytheistic idol worshippers. For example, recall Paul's experience (recorded in Acts 19) in Ephesus as he locked horns with the worshippers of the fertility goddess, Artemis. The silversmiths, who made a good living selling expensive religious trinkets to tourists, realized that if Paul was successful he might very well undermine the economy of the city. The silversmiths incited a riot against Paul in Ephesus, and he was obliged to flee the city during that riot. Recall further that Paul wrote his epistle to the Romans in Corinth. Since the temple of the fertility goddess Aphrodite was built on the Acrocorinth (the great acropolis of Corinth) Paul would probably have seen it every time he went out his door. It was obviously in his mind as he began to write, and Professor Jeremy Townsley explains this well:

> *The importance of the goddess religions in the Greco-Roman period cannot be underestimated. During Paul's missionary travels, the goddess religions were having a wide resurgence, and [A.T.]Fear notes that while "mystery religions in general*

were not a focus of Christian polemic, Attis and Cybele on the other hand appear to have been a favorite target for the invective of Christian writers." Temples dedicated to Cybele/Attis, Artemis, Aphrodite, Demeter and Venus were in most large cities of the region. The temple to Artemis in Ephesus was claimed to be the largest building in the world and one of the Seven Wonders, and as will be described later, Acts 19 describes a conflict between Paul and the followers of Artemis in Ephesus. Strabo (somewhat dubiously) claimed that the temple to Aphrodite in Corinth had more than 1,000 temple prostitutes and it was this business that made the city rich. In Rome, the Cybele/ Attis temple was built in the heart of the city on one of the Seven Hills of Rome. The Roman temple to another goddess, Aphrodite, was on another of these hills and the official sanctions that had prevented citizens from fully participating in the priestly rituals were lifted in the mid-first century. In addition, Cybele's image was printed on some Roman coins. Two major city festivals, the Day of Blood and the Megalensia, were organized around Cybele and Attis, and a statue of Cybele presided over the public

> *games. Roller describes the worship of*
> *Cybele as central to Roman life.* "Paul, the
> Goddess Religions and Queer Sects:
> Romans 1:23-28." Jeremy Townsley. SBL
> vol.130, #4 (Winter 2011) p. 717.

These fertility cults were powerful and pervasive throughout the Mediterranean world, although they were simultaneously viewed by many Romans as scandalous. They had cult prostitutes, of course, but more disturbing to both Paul and ordinary citizens were some of the worship practices, which involved not only deliberate sex reversal, but more disturbingly, self-mutilation. That is, the men would present themselves as women, and the women as men in orgiastic worship. This was anathema to the Roman culture of male honor and virtue, as well as to the Jewish sensibility. Worse, however, was the fact that self-mutilation and castration were a part of the lurid worship, which is Paul's reference to receiving in their persons the due penalty for their error.

Take for example, the worship of Dionysus as he was known to the Greeks, or Bacchus, as he was known to the Romans. The god Dionysus was believed to have been born the son of Zeus and Semele. His mother died, and he was disguised as a girl to keep him safe from the goddess Hera. This ruse was unsuccessful, and he was sent to an island inhabited only by women. He was dressed in women's clothing, and was raised essentially as a woman. You may notice that when you see statues of him, he looks like an androgynous youth. He has long, curly hair and is dressed in feminine, flowing garments. His body looks rather soft and feminine. Dionysus, or Bacchus in Roman parlance, was an important god in Greek and Roman culture. He was the god of grape cultivation, wine, fertility, ritual madness, theatre, and androgyny. You may have heard of "Bacchanalian orgies." The Roman historian, Titus Livius Patavinus, who lived from about 64BC to 17AD, and with whose writings Paul would have been familiar, describes the religious rites from about 200 years earlier in terms echoed by Paul in Romans 1…

> *When they were heated with wine and the nightly commingling of men and women, those of tender age with their seniors, had extinguished all sense of modesty, debaucheries of every kind commenced; each had pleasures at hand to satisfy the lust he was most prone to. Nor was the mischief confined to the promiscuous intercourse of men and women; false witness, the forging of seals and testaments, and false informations, all*

proceeded from the same source, as also poisonings and murders of families where the bodies could not even be found for burial. Many crimes were committed by treachery; most by violence, which was kept secret, because the cries of those who were being violated or murdered could not be heard owing to the noise of drums and cymbals. (Livy, The History of Rome. Book 39.8)

The objection here is not that two men or two women are living in a peaceful and loving relationship. Rather, this is a compendium of every variant of ritualized evil, including orgiastic sex, pederasty, gang rape, forgeries, conspiracies, poisonings, and murders. It comports very nearly with Paul's outraged objections. In less dramatic language, we have the assessment of Dr. Catherine Kroeger, who was a New Testament scholar specializing in ancient Greek culture. A professor at the conservative evangelical Gordon-Conwell Theological Seminary, she wrote:

Sex reversal was a specific distinctive of the Dionysiac cult and by the second century A.D. was considered to be indispensable to the religion. Men wore veils and long hair as signs of their dedication to the god, while women used the unveiling and shorn hair to indicate their devotion. Men masqueraded as women, and in a rare vase painting from Corinth a woman is dressed in satyr pants equipped with the male organ. Thus she dances before Dionysus, a deity who had been raised as a girl and was himself called male-female and 'sham-man.' The sex exchange that characterized the cults of such great goddesses as Cybele, the Syrian goddess, and Artemis of Ephesus was more grisly. Males voluntarily castrated themselves and assumed women's garments. A relief from Rome shows a high priest of Cybele. The castrated priest wears veil, necklaces, earrings and feminine dress. He is considered to have exchanged his sexual identity and to have become a she-priest." (Catherine Kroeger JETS 30/1 March 1987 p. 37).

Notice that in Dr. Kroeger's assessment, she describes not only the sex-reversal that was typical of Dionysus or Bacchus, but also the self-mutilation and castration which were part of the worship. We see similar aspects in the worship of Aphrodite, a Greek goddess derived from the fertility goddess, Astarte, whom you may remember from the Old Testament as tempting the Israelites away from the worship of God. Athens and Corinth were major centers of worship of Aphrodite, as was Rome where she was known as Venus.

The second century historian, Lucian, wrote *The Syrian Goddess*. He describes the worship of Cybele on the "Day of Blood" which was also practiced in Rome. In Corinth, Cybele was worshipped as Aphrodite. In Rome, she was worshipped officially as the "Magna Mater," or the Great Mother, with an imposing and prominent temple on the Palatine Hill. It might be interesting to note that Cybele was also worshipped in Paul's hometown of Tarsus. The "Day of Blood" was on the Roman calendar annually for March 24, and any cursory research will yield an abundance of material on the castrated priests (called Galli) who attended the worship of Cybele, as well as the orgy of sex and blood that attended the rites of March 24 each year. Here is Lucian's description, from sections 50 and 51:

> *On certain days a multitude flocks into the temple, and the Galli in great numbers, sacred as they are, perform the ceremonies of the men and gash their arms and turn their backs to be lashed. Many bystanders play on the pipes the while many beat drums; others sing divine and sacred songs. All this performance takes place*

outside the temple, and those engaged in the ceremony enter not into the temple. During these days they are made Galli. As the Galli sing and celebrate their orgies, frenzy falls on many of them and many who had come as mere spectators afterwards are found to have committed the great act [self-castration]. I will narrate what they do. Any young man who has resolved on this action, strips off his clothes, and with a loud shout bursts into the midst of the crowd, and picks up a sword from a number of swords which I suppose have been kept ready for many years for this purpose. He takes it and castrates himself and then runs wild through the city, bearing in his hands what he has cut off. He casts it into any house at will, and from this house he receives women's raiment and

> ***It makes as much sense to use Romans 1 to prohibit all homosexual love as it does to use the prohibitions on adultery to eliminate all heterosexual love.***

> *ornaments. Thus they act during their ceremonies of castration.*

I hope all this is beginning to make sense. Paul writes with deep disgust and vehemence in Romans 1 against the excesses of the fertility goddess worship. By reviewing other ancient texts, we can understand why. To apply this passage to homosexuals in general is either ignorant, dishonest, or both. If this scripture were about ordinary homosexuals, then homosexuals as a general class would all have to be idol worshippers, would have to receive in their own physical bodies a penalty for their behavior, and would have to be thoroughly evil, fulfilling the description of Romans 1. This is not the case, because Paul is describing fertility cult worshippers, particularly the Galli and the temple prostitutes. He is not writing about LGBTQI people who simply wish to live in loving and committed relationships. He is writing about entrenched idol worship accompanied by orgiastic sex, prostitution, and mutilation.

Conservatives might suggest that if this passage were interpreted as a prohibition of homosexuality in general, then that would automatically eliminate the excesses described by Paul. But there are two problems with this. The first is that this would involve a prohibition that is broader than the passage states. It makes as much sense to use Romans 1 to prohibit all homosexual love as it does to use the prohibitions on adultery to eliminate all heterosexual love. Certainly prohibiting heterosexual relationships would also prohibit adultery, but this prohibition is too broad. Similarly, to broaden this passage to a wholesale indictment of homosexuality would be to misunderstand the passage, and in light of current scholarship it would be a willful misunderstanding. The second problem is that since sexual orientation and identity are formed in the womb, the only way to eliminate LGBTQI orientation and identity would be to eliminate LGBTQI people. This was Hitler's idea.

Who Was Worshipping the Female Fertility Goddesses?

Not all worshippers of the female fertility goddesses approved of the more extreme manifestations of the cult, and obviously not many became priests who castrated themselves. Yet, the female fertility goddesses provided a place for LGBTQI persons to belong, and to create an important, meaningful identity. Some LGBTQI people were probably driven toward the fertility cults because these provided a context for their personal story and identity that was bold, highly valued, and affirming in a culture that marginalized LGBTQI people. Probably many who castrated themselves in a frenzy of cultic activity regretted it later, as indicated by some historic sources. The most tragic part is the evil and excess that attended this identity as a "Gallus," or castrated priest.

Wouldn't it be better if the Church could give a powerful context of love for all people, including LGBTQI people? Wouldn't it be better if we could affirm what many already know: "God created you with the sexual identity and orientation you have. You may have a journey to figure out what that truly is, but whatever it is we will celebrate with you God's goodness and wisdom in creating you as you are?" In this way, we could allow people to figure out who they are in a context of holy love. And in this same context, they could marry a partner that is right for them. Or if it is better for them, they can choose to be like so many single people who love God and remain celibate.

So Did Paul Approve of Homosexuality?

No one truly knows how Paul felt about homosexuality as we know it. It is easy to assume that Paul would not approve of homosexuality, and yet he only wrote about its excesses in terms of pederasty, cult prostitution, and ritualized temple orgies. It is interesting to note that he mentions in Romans 1:32 "God's decree that those who practice *such things* (emphasis added) deserve to die." In Romans 1, Paul is dealing with cult prostitution and ritualized temple orgies. In referring to God's decree, he obviously is referencing Leviticus 20:13. This supports the notion that Paul believed Leviticus 20:13 dealt with the same problem he addressed in Romans 1: not simple LGBTQI relations but male temple prostitution, orgies and all the other aspects of cultic sex we have already addressed in the Old and New Testament contexts of fertility God worship.

In Paul's world, the homosexual objections he raises are always bound up with issues of violent and orgiastic cult worship, slavery, and pederasty. As we read the New Testament, it is difficult for us to separate the simple, committed love of a homosexual couple from the violent and exploitative aspects of sexuality which the scriptures condemn. Paul is writing a letter to the Church in first century Rome. Within the specific context of that letter we can draw wisdom, teaching and good theology. But we cannot take Paul out of his context. We cannot ask Paul what he thinks about epigenetics. We cannot ask Paul what he would think about two Christians living in a committed and loving homosexual relationship, and the Bible never addresses this. We can only ask Paul what he thinks of homosexual practices that are addressed in scripture, as commonly practiced in the Greco-Roman world. Romans, I Corinthians and I Timothy give us a good answer to that. We all agree with Paul that orgiastic and violent cult worship, pederasty and sexual slavery are wrong. That isn't really the question. But that is the only question the Bible can answer, because that is the inescapable context of the biblical world.

LGBTQI people were living quietly in committed relationships in the ancient world; it is just that this is not the kind of homosexual relationship scripture addresses. Scripture addresses rape, pederasty and cult prostitution. Therefore, we have to be courageous enough to ask: in our current context, with our increased scientific and sociological understanding of LGBTQI people, what is the right thing? Telling them to pray to become straight is not a loving, kind, or credible option. Telling them that they will have to either be celibate or be damned isn't either. Some heterosexual people may be willing to simply be dismissive of the entire LGBTQI population as if they do not matter. I do not think that is the way of Jesus. That is not the way civilized people behave, and that is not the way *we* behave. When we simply dismiss Christian LGBTQI people in terms that sound like, "turn or burn," we may be in more danger of judgment by Jesus than they.

No one would wish for a return to an evil and abusive system of sexual exploitation. We can all agree on this. But Paul's argument, again, is a blunt instrument. It is certainly a step forward in holiness to insist that men preying sexually on weaker men and boys should be forbidden. And it is positive to encourage married people to channel their affections toward delight in one another rather than resort to fornication and adultery.

Paul's context for teaching on adultery was very different than our context. Paul's context is as repugnant to us as it was to him. But Paul was not addressing loving and committed

> *It is time to let go of the wishful thinking that everyone can be straight if they pray, believe and try really, really hard.*

LGBTQI relationships, nor did Paul know about genetics and epigenetics. We do. Isn't it time we stopped treating people who are born LGBTQI as if they were the moral equivalent of unrepentant adulterers and thieves? Like straight people, LGBTQI people need the grace and forgiveness of

Jesus Christ, and they need the redeeming community of the Church. But they do not need to repent of the orientation God gave them. Now we know from scientific research that sexual orientation is fixed in the waters of the womb, not in the waters of baptism.

Of course, when science and scripture clash, it can take a hundred years for some conservatives to either die out or to accept the science. But does anyone really want to be that kind of conservative? It is time to let go of the wishful thinking that everyone can be straight if they pray, believe and try really, really hard.

I Corinthians 6:9-10 (NRSV)

Do you not know that wrongdoers will not inherit the kingdom of God? Do not be deceived! Fornicators, idolaters, adulterers, male prostitutes, sodomites, thieves, the greedy, drunkards, revilers, robbers—none of these will inherit the kingdom of God.

I Timothy 1:9-10 (NRSV)

This means understanding that the law is laid down not for the innocent but for the lawless and disobedient, for the godless and sinful, for the unholy and profane, for those who kill their father or mother, for murderers, fornicators, sodomites,

*slave traders, liars, perjurers, and whatever else
is contrary to the sound teaching.*

For a few minutes, we will deal with these two
texts together because they are extremely similar.
Both texts are said to be written by Paul, both
provide a list of unrighteous behaviors, and both
lists include the word, *arsenokoitai(s)*. The
Corinthian text says that those who practice these
behaviors will not inherit the kingdom of God, and
the Timothy text says these behaviors are outside
God's law.

Scholars agree that Paul wrote both Romans,
which we looked at a moment ago, and I
Corinthians. Scholars do not agree whether Paul
wrote I Timothy; some say yes, some say maybe,
some say no. Whether Paul wrote I Timothy or
not, and I am among those who believe he did, the
list of sinful behaviors is consistent with Paul's
thought. You may remember that Paul's eyesight
was terrible and he had others actually pen letters
for him; whether these were always dictated word
for word is an interesting question. Regardless, the
theology is consistently Pauline. Some people like
to isolate to Paul certain cultural biases which we
now find odious, such as his view of women. It
may well be that Paul was the champion of such a
religious viewpoint, but regardless of authorship,
these letters are canonized. They are sacred

scripture for Christians. But this does not mean they are infallible, and it does not mean that they may not be culture bound. We have seen many examples of scriptural writings which are culture bound and could have given many more. We conservatives do not like to acknowledge that any scripture is culture bound; we prefer not to talk about it. But unless we want to adopt a flat earth science, stop shaving, and re-start the slave industry, we must admit that this category exists. The question is whether Paul's view of homosexuality is culture bound, and I think it is.

First, we need to translate Paul's Greek. Sometimes this task is not easy, and this is definitely one of those times. The way we translate Greek, and enrich our understanding of the nuances of it, is to see how a certain Greek word has been used in other places. By looking at the way a word is used in multiple contexts, we can enlarge and enrich our understanding of its nuances of meaning.

Unfortunately, we do not have that luxury with the word Paul used in these two passages, because the word translated here as "sodomites" is the Greek word *arsenokoitai(s)*. Now, it seems quite likely that the practice referred to in these passages involves sodomy; the problem is that it seems to involve not sodomy in general but pederasty in particular. *Arsenokoitai(s)* is a word Paul coined himself instead of using the ordinary Greek words for homosexuals. There is certainly nothing wrong with making up new words. It shows erudition and creativity. But when we are trying to excavate all the possible nuances of that word by examining all the possible contexts in which that word is used, we are at a loss because Paul's unique word is used in the New Testament only these two times. It appears to many that his new word is derived specifically from the Septuagint (the Greek translation of the Hebrew Bible with which Paul would have been quite familiar) translation of Leviticus 18:22 and Leviticus 20:13. In the Greek, they use the words *arsenos* (man) and *koiten* (beds). So the literal translation would be "man beds." And that may be fully and exactly what Paul means, but there are problems with this.

This term may refer to every form of homosexual act or it may not. Upon close examination it appears not. We have already talked about four kinds of homosexual activity recognized in the ancient world: men raping men to demonstrate dominance, men having sex with boys which was called pederasty, men having sex with both male and female slaves, and men having sex with male temple prostitutes. All of this was antithetical to the teachings of Judaism, and it was repugnant to Paul; it is also repugnant to us. These kinds of sexual abuse, however, were accepted as more or less normal in the ancient world. Paul was trying his best to help non-Jewish converts to see that this behavior was categorically out of bounds. All of us would agree.

But if we want to know what the word *arsenokoitai* really means, we have to look at how it is used in different contexts. If you are inclined to look it up, it is interesting to see what Philo of Alexandria, Paul's contemporary Jewish philosopher and historian, thought about the question of *arsenos koiten*. (See Philo, The Special Laws, III VII 37-42.) Philo produces a commentary on the Old Testament law of Moses. In commenting about the passages we reviewed from Leviticus, Philo describes in great detail what he sees as pederasty, or the violation of men having sex with boys who were cult prostitutes: "Moreover, another evil, much greater than that which we have already mentioned, has made its way among and been let loose upon cities, namely, the love of boys. . ." Philo goes on to describe vividly, though not lewdly, the homosexual excesses of shrine prostitution. It is important to note that Philo's interpretation of *arsenos koiten* is men who have sex with boys who are engaged in temple prostitution. This comports almost exactly with the meaning of both the Corinthians and the Timothy passages: cult prostitution and pederasty.

It also suggests that Philo's understanding of Leviticus is that it deals with pederasty and male temple prostitution. Martin Luther, the architect of the Protestant Reformation, was not positively inclined toward homosexuality; but he viewed the Leviticus passages, as well as the passages in I Corinthians and I Timothy as referring exclusively to pederasty, and he translated the passages accordingly.

Let's look at the operative Greek words in the Corinthians text: *pornoi, eidololatrai, moichoi, malachoi*, and *arsenokoitai*. We will use Bauer's 2nd Edition Greek-English Lexicon which is a standard, conservative work. *Pornoi* means male prostitutes (it has the masculine plural ending). *Eidololatrai* means idol worshippers, *moichoi* means adulterers, *malachoi* when referring to persons means catamites, or men or boys who allow themselves to be misused sexually, *arsenokoitai* means a male who practices homosexuality, or a pederast, or a sodomite. Notice that the words *malachoi* and *arsenokoitai* have multiple meanings. So a perfectly acceptable translation of *malachoi* is catamites or boy prostitutes, and a prescribed translation for *arsenokoitai* is pederast. So the sentence could quite accurately be rendered: "Male prostitutes, idolators, adulterers, catamites, pederasts who abuse them,…" In other words, this is about men having sex with boys. Look at the common thread in this sentence construction: it fits perfectly the context of worship in the female fertility cults. There is a connection here between male prostitutes, idol worshippers, catamites and pederasts. These are among the same activities described above in our discussion of the Romans text. This is not about Adam and Steve having a committed relationship. What is condemned here is ritual prostitution and the ritual sexual abuse of minors. Catamites, by the way, were castrated when they were quite young (a horrible procedure done without drugs or anesthetics) in order to preserve their effeminate delicacy. Of course, they grew up anyway; hence, catamites began as children and continued their sexually abused roles through adulthood.

Now let's look at the operative words in the Timothy text. You will notice that they seem to be grouped in twos and threes, each modifying the other. This is a literary device we often see in the Psalms and in wisdom literature such as Proverbs. We are not surprised that Paul, so steeped in scripture, would use a similar literary device. In verse 9, "the lawless and the disobedient" pair together and modify each other. The "godless and the sinful" likewise pair. The "unholy and the profane" form a pair. Killers of fathers, mothers and murderers form a triad. What about the next triad? As it is currently translated it is the only triad where each term does not modify the others: fornicators, sodomites, slave traders. But let's move on, because we get another pair: liars and perjurers. Doesn't it seem odd that these descriptors all fall into pairs and triads except the one dealing with homosexuality? Let's look at the Greek words. They are *pornois, arsenokoitais*, and *andrapodistais*. We have already seen from a similar listing in I Corinthians that *pornois* is prostitutes. The second word is *arsenokoitais* which might mean pederasts or homosexuals. The third word is *andrapodistais* which means slave dealer or kidnapper. Think about the role that pimps played with prostitutes in the ancient world, and which they still play. Often the designation of pimp is just another word for someone who enslaves prostitutes. So this triad could well be interpreted: boys who are cult prostitutes, the men who pay for them, and those who enslave them.

The New American Bible Revised Edition has the following footnote for I Corinthians 6:9 which they also apply to I Timothy 1:10. "The Greek word translated as boy prostitutes may refer to catamites, i.e., boys or young men who were kept for purposes of prostitution, a practice not uncommon in the Greco-Roman world. In Greek mythology this was the function of Ganymede, the 'cupbearer of the gods,' whose Latin name was

Catamitus. The term translated sodomites refers to adult males who indulged in homosexual practices with such boys. See similar condemnations of such practices in Rom 1:26–27; 1 Tm 1:10."

So the NAB translates all these passages, including Romans 1, in terms of pederasty and prostitution. Another example is the NASB Interlinear Greek English New Testament by Alfred Marshall, 1984, (Zondervan) which translates *arsenokoitais* in I Timothy 1:10 as "pederasts." In William Barclay's 1956 Commentary on I Timothy, Barclay writes a paragraph on what valuable slaves, "beautiful male youths" were, and how much they were in demand by slave dealers who were not above kidnapping. Like Martin Luther of old, many current commentaries translate *arsenokoitais* as pederasty. Strangely, some translations translate *arsenokoitais* as pederasts in one place, and translate the same word as homosexuals in another. There is no textual reason for this; it is simply an understandable cultural bias on the part of the translators.

Once again, this passage is about the world of cult prostitution, pederasty and enslavement. We would all agree that it is good for the Christian scriptures to outlaw such behavior. But this passage is not about LGBTQI people who simply want to live in a committed and loving relationship. It is about prostitution, sexual slavery and abuse.

What Did Jesus Say?

Jesus said nothing negative about LGBTQI people or practice. This is important for all of us. If homosexuality were the sin many conservatives think it

> *Jesus said nothing negative about LGBTQI people.*

is, it would make sense for Jesus to have discussed this. As we have seen, it was certainly not because homosexuality was uncommon. The entire Roman world was familiar with homosexuality and it was rather openly practiced. Romans and their culture were very much present throughout Israel during this time. But Jesus uttered not one word of teaching against LGBTQI people. Some say this is because the traditional Jewish teaching was already clear, although it certainly was not adhered to in the Roman world. Jesus, however, may have given a liberal and sympathetic teaching about LGBTQI people in Matthew 19:3-12.

Matthew 19:3-12 (NRSV)

3Some Pharisees came to him, and to test him they asked, "Is it lawful for a man to divorce his wife for any cause?" 4 He answered, "Have you not read that the one who made them at the beginning 'made them male and female,' 5 and said, 'For this reason a man shall leave his father and mother and be joined to his wife, and the two shall become one flesh'? 6 So they are no longer two, but one flesh. Therefore what God has joined together, let no one separate." 7 They said to him, "Why then did Moses command us to give a certificate of dismissal and to divorce her?" 8 He said to them, "It was because you were so hard-hearted that Moses allowed you to divorce your wives, but from the beginning it was not so. 9 And I say to you, whoever divorces his wife, except for unchastity, and marries another commits adultery.10 His disciples said to him, "If such is the case of a man with his wife, it is better not to marry." 11 But he said to them, "Not everyone can accept this teaching, but only those to whom it is given. 12 For there are eunuchs who have been so from birth, and there are eunuchs who have been made eunuchs by others, and there are eunuchs

> *who have made themselves eunuchs for the*
> *sake of the kingdom of heaven. Let anyone*
> *accept this who can."*

I have included this entire pericope for two reasons. The first is that by Jesus' teaching on marriage, some conservatives believe Jesus indirectly condemned homosexual marriage. This is both illogical and untrue. Jesus' teaching here is about divorce; he references the norm of marriage from Genesis in order to render his teaching on marriage as a life-long commitment. It is undoubtedly true that the norm for marriage was heterosexual. By referring to that norm, Jesus does not comment upon homosexual marriage. That would be like saying that since the current norm is for brides to wear white, only women wearing white can become brides. That is illogical.

More important is the reference to eunuchs. Not all eunuchs were homosexual, but they were generally assumed to be for good reason, which a quick Google search will confirm. In verse 12, Jesus refers to those who are born eunuchs. Here, he may be referring literally to men born without testicles, but at a rate of 1 man in 6 million, this condition is so rare it is doubtful that anyone in Judah had heard of such a condition, let alone experienced it. Jesus was more likely referring to men who are eunuchs figuratively, which was a common reference of the time to homosexual men. The second reference is to males who were made eunuchs, usually against their will, so they could serve in palaces, harems, and royal courts. Again, these men were assumed to function as homosexuals after their surgery, though there were exceptions. Then there are those who have made themselves eunuchs for the kingdom of heaven. This may suggest that some men literally underwent castration for religious service, but the early Church understood this to be figurative, in the sense that some men forgo marriage in order to serve the kingdom. The figurative meaning for this third reference supports a figurative meaning for the first reference. If so, Jesus is saying in his typically indirect manner of teaching, "Not everyone is straight. It's okay."

While we are on the subject of eunuchs, Acts 8:28-40 tells us of the Ethiopian eunuch, who was a very early Christian convert. He was eager to understand the scriptures, and the Holy Spirit instructed Philip to go to him. The eunuch was baptized that very day by the guidance of the Holy Spirit. As mentioned, eunuchs were assumed to be homosexual. This man provides a good example and focal point for the agency of the Holy Spirit in actively bringing LGBTQI people into the Church. In addition, note Isaiah 56:3-5, which announces

God's inclusion of those who are sexually "other."
God welcomes and blesses those who choose him.

*For thus says the Lord: To the eunuchs who keep
my sabbaths, who choose the things that please
me and hold fast my covenant, I will give, in my
house and within my walls, a monument and a
name better than sons and daughters; I will give
them an everlasting name that shall not be cut off.*

The Golden Rule and the Great Two-Fold Commandment

Matthew 7:12 (NRSV) *In everything do to others
as you would have them do to you; for this is the
law and the prophets.*
Matthew 22:36-40 (NRSV) *'Teacher, which
commandment in the law is the greatest?' He said
to him, 'You shall love the Lord your God with all
your heart, and with all your soul, and with all
your mind.' This is the greatest and first
commandment. And a second is like it: 'You shall
love your neighbor as yourself.' On these two
commandments hang all the law and the
prophets.*

Some scriptures are more important than others;
they sum up the essence of all the other scriptures.
As Christians, we believe that the commandments
to love God and neighbor are the greatest. They

provide a hermeneutic or superstructure through which to view and interpret all the others. They help us to rightly interpret scriptures that are culture bound. These two scriptures are centered on love. The Great Commandment directs our greatest love toward God and then our next love towards neighbor. The Golden Rule helps us begin to understand how to love our neighbor. Multiple New Testament passages repeat this "highest ethic" view of holy love.

There was a time when we believed that homosexuality was merely a powerful lie which needed to be dispelled. Many still see it this way. The thinking for conservatives was that the most loving option was to warn homosexuals that they had chosen a wrong path and to encourage them to embrace heterosexuality. It is important to note that for most people, the conservative approach was characterized by holy love of God and neighbor: honoring what they believed were the teachings of God and encouraging their neighbors to enjoy the blessings of heterosexuality. Even when these folks are shrill, demanding, and screaming hate language, they believe they are motivated by love of God and neighbor, or that if they have crossed the line into hating, they are righteously mirroring God's hatred. Thus, some believe that treating LGBTQI people with hate honors their love for God; they believe it is also a form of tough love for their LGBTQI neighbors. They can say with a twisted but clear conscience that if they themselves had chosen to "go and be gay" they would want someone to show them enough tough love to scare them back onto the right path. But would they? They cannot know, because they cannot fully imagine what it is like to be LGBTQI. They assume that they would have a true freedom of choice that actually is not available.

So there are multiple fatal flaws to this logic. The first, as we have seen, is that the anti-gay scriptures are culture bound and misinterpreted. We cannot know what the scriptural writers thought about LGBTQI people who wanted to live in loving and committed relationships, because they deal with people who are involved in pederasty, gang rape, and temple prostitution. Moreover, ancient people did not understand genetics and epigenetics as we do. They had little means of seeing homosexuality as anything other than a moral deviation. More compelling is the fact that we now know that LGBTQI people do not choose their orientation and identity; it is indelibly imprinted in the womb. God made them the way they are, and as Psalm 139 says, all of us are "fearfully and wonderfully made."

Another flaw is the false assumption that people have a choice about their identity and orientation. They don't. And now we know the conservative view isn't just a lie, it is a vicious lie. It is vicious to tell people that if they cannot change their identity and orientation so it matches ours, and the other 95% of the population, then they are appropriately rejected by God and neighbor. Imagine the enormous weight of being misunderstood by 95% of the population. That is burden enough. Should we compound that difficult fact by telling them, erroneously, they are rejected by God? If we are in doubt about the best ways to express our love for LGBTQI people, it would be appropriate to ask them. They are probably the best judges of that. Hurling abuse at people is not a form of "love" that decent people practice.

> *Hurling abuse at people is not a form of "love" that decent people practice.*

Harm to LGBTQI Neighbors

Studies indicate that LGBTQI youth are two to seven times more likely to commit suicide than their straight peers. Adult homosexuals are at much greater risk for depression and suicide than heterosexuals. Why is this? Religious conservatives tend to think it is because they are living in sin, and sin leads to despair. But health care professionals believe it is because LGBTQI people live with a much higher level of bullying, social isolation and rejection from society, even from their own families. Although I agree that living in sin leads to despair, I do not think being LGBTQI is a sin. But when the Church and society treat LGBTQI people as though they were inherently sinful, loathsome, and disgusting, this certainly would be a breeding ground for despair since LGBTQI people cannot choose their orientation. The Church and society tell them to change, and their experience is that they cannot change. Worse, since Church and society insist they change, many LGBTQI people blame themselves for not becoming straight. Telling people they are rightly rejected by God and society unless they change what they cannot change is not loving. It is extraordinarily cruel.

Conservatives are responsible before God for the harm they do to their LGBTQI neighbors. Those who believe they love God by oppressing their neighbors bear a close resemblance to the Pharisees and Sadducees who hounded Jesus to his death as a way of demonstrating their love for God. They do not resemble the love and grace of

Jesus Christ. We now know that "turn or burn" does not apply to LGBTQI people, but it may apply to those who persecute them. We can't even say, "Father, forgive us, we did not know" because now we do.

If LGBTQI people cannot choose a straight orientation and identity, it is the antithesis of love to insist that they are unacceptable to God until they do so. Love says, "I see you as you are. I accept you as you are. I value you as you are. Let's worship the Lord together!" No less than heterosexuals, LGBTQI people need forgiveness of sin and reconciliation with God and neighbor. When we attempt to make them turn upon their own identities in order to be accepted by the Church, we set in motion an impossible dilemma. If they pretend they are straight when they are not, they cannot be authentically the persons God created them to be. In order to find acceptance with God and the Church in this case, they would have to turn against themselves. If they refuse to pretend to be straight, then we communicate that they are unrepentant sinners scorned or pitied by the Church and rejected by God.

Fornication and Homosexual Marriage

Although the scripture is ambiguous about homosexuality, it is not ambiguous about sex outside marriage. Sex outside the commitment of marriage is fornication. Until gay marriage was legalized, homosexuals were in a difficult position in terms of sin and righteousness. It was certainly possible for homosexual couples to live in loving, committed, and monogamous relationships. In many cases, they presented themselves to the world as "roomates," as we discussed in Chapter 1. But these relationships were not blessed by the Church, and they were not recognized by society.

The Church and society lend a tremendous stabilizing force upon marriage, and this stabilizing support has not been available to LGBTQI persons. Are people who live under the voluntary constraints of a loving, committed, monogamous relationship committing fornication when it is impossible for them to marry? I do not believe this is what the scriptures envision when fornication is discussed. Nevertheless, until homosexual marriage was legalized, LGBTQI couples had no choice but to live under this ambiguous cloud. Without homosexual marriage, the Church had no reasonable expectations of LGBTQI people. Recognizing this, many LGBTQI people dismissed the Church and its moral authority as irrelevant.

Some conservatives fear that allowing homosexuals to marry will cause a decline in the population, as in "what if everybody did that?" In previous centuries, there was a strong emphasis on the need for people to reproduce in order to make their countries more populous and thus stronger. The opposite concern is prevalent in most countries today. Nevertheless, without gay marriage we can assume two things: either homosexuals are not marrying anyone, and thus they are not producing children anyway, or they are pretending to be straight and duping their mates into believing they are appropriate partners when they are not. Most of us know someone whose marriage crumbled because a spouse who was homosexual was pretending, or hoping, to be straight. This is devastating for families, and the Church should not encourage these harmful lies.

Other conservatives fear that allowing homosexuals to marry will encourage more people to be gay. This concern operates under the incorrect assumption that people choose to be straight or homosexual. But being gay is not a choice which becomes more attractive when social opprobrium is lifted. It is a fact of life which becomes okay when social opprobrium and religious censure are lifted. People who are heterosexual in orientation and identity can no more become homosexual than homosexuals can become heterosexual, although Greg noted that heterosexuals can function homosexually under constrained same sex conditions such as prison.

Some conservatives fear that allowing homosexuals to marry will anger God. I think conservatives sometimes misunderstand what makes God angry. It makes God angry when the poor, the disadvantaged, and the weak are mistreated and abused by the strong and powerful. LGBTQI people are a tiny minority who have been abused by society for centuries, and the Church has shared in this guilt. Treating people with lovingkindness is the way of Christ. Ponder Matthew 25: "As you did it unto the least of these my brothers and sisters, you did it unto me."

> *Conservatives sometimes misunderstand what makes God angry...*

By allowing homosexual marriage, and teaching "celibacy in singleness and faithfulness in marriage," the Church would actually increase its moral authority in matters of sexual practice.

Under the current system, the Church unrealistically tells LGBTQI people that they must either figure out a way to be straight or to live single, sexless, and celibate. That is simply untenable for most LGBTQI people; therefore, many dismiss the Church's teaching and authority completely, in much the same way that the Church dismisses them as willful sinners.

Heterosexuals have many sinful sexual impulses which are quite natural. But through marriage the Church offers them a way to channel their sexuality into building a stable home with a permanent mate. This channels heterosexuality in a positive direction. In the same way, the Church could help LGBTQI people channel their sexuality in a positive direction by introducing them to Jesus Christ and teaching them the model of celibacy in singleness and faithfulness in marriage. While it is certainly to be expected that not all LGBTQI Christians will practice this kind of moral purity, we understand that not all straight Christians do, either. We can, however, reasonably teach this, and ask everyone to adhere to it.

Questions for Reflection and Discussion

1. What were the primary concerns of the author(s) of Romans, I Corinthians and I Timothy in dealing with homosexuality?

2. How was sexuality in the ancient world driven by power differentials? How is sexuality in our nation today driven by power differentials? Is this the same for women as for men? How do laws, social censure and religious teaching help regulate this?

3. Do you know any LGBTQI persons? Do they match Paul's description in Roman's 1? Whom do you think Paul has in mind as he is writing?

4. How were the fertility cults of Paul's day related to fertility cults in the Old Testament period? In what ways do writers of the Old and New Testaments share similar concerns? What are these concerns?

5. Does the Church today have a "turn or burn" message for LGBTQI people?

6. How does the New Testament ethic of love illuminate the question of how to treat LGBTQI people?

7. Are LGBTQI people helped or hurt by religious opprobrium and disapproval?

For Further Research: Do an internet search on "cult temple worship in the ancient world."

8

Conclusion

From ancient times until recently, heterosexuals had the privilege of telling the story of what it means to be homosexual in spite of the fact that they knew little about it. From the standpoint of heterosexuality, LGBTQI people were usually viewed as immoral and self-degrading. We believed that everyone was straight, and that those who thought they were not had somehow believed a lie. Or less charitably, we believed they were simply perverse. There was a turning point with the Stonewall riots in 1969 and the "Gay Liberation." Homosexuals began to find their voices and tell their own stories. As LGBTQI people began to speak up, we learned that they are our neighbors and friends, our sons and

Our sexual orientation and identity are determined in the waters of the womb, not in the waters of baptism.

daughters. All kinds of research began to tell us more about homosexuality from a sociological and biological viewpoint, rather than from an anecdotal heterosexual viewpoint. We had always thought that LGBTQI people could become straight if they loved God enough. Now we know that being straight is not a result of loving God. Our sexual orientation and identity are determined in the waters of the womb, not in the waters of baptism.

This led to a rediscovery of what scripture actually says about homosexuality, and this is difficult for conservatives. In this book, we have spent a lot of time looking at how scripture is interpreted. Inevitably, scripture primarily addresses its own time and place, often transcending both. Figuring out what part transcends culture, and what part is culture bound is sometimes extremely difficult. We don't want to let go of a single word that God intended to be transcendent, and yet we do not want to hobble people unnecessarily with laws, customs, and concepts that are culturally bound to the ancient world.

The way we usually discern God's direction is by looking at scripture, tradition, reason and experience. When scripture and tradition are united on a subject, that usually is a strong indication of God's direction. It is extremely hard to redress a rare wrong supported by these two powerful sources. This was the case with geocentrism, slavery, and women's rights. Neither the writers of scripture, nor the Church could see that they were culture bound in these areas. Teachings that had once been a progressive improvement in society had ossified into an anchor keeping us from moving into further expressions of love and justice. Gradually, reason and experience overturned scripture and tradition on these subjects. But because scripture and tradition were united in these cases, it was extremely difficult as the conservative gave way to the progressive. Change was slow and stomach-turning, resulting in imprisonments, executions, riots and wars.

Scripture and tradition seem united in viewing male homosexuality as a sin; lesbianism is virtually unaddressed in scripture despite some inaccurate and sweeping translations. As we examine it more closely, we see that tradition is actually more strongly positioned against homosexuality than scripture. There are few scriptures which address homosexuality, and with the possible exception of Leviticus, all are addressing gang rape, pederasty, or cult prostitution. It is unclear whether Leviticus is concerned with pederasty and cult prostitution; Martin Luther thought Leviticus dealt with pederasty and translated it accordingly, as did Philo of Alexandria. Now that more biblical scholars are looking at scripture more extensively on this subject, the translations as well as the commentaries will be translated more narrowly and more precisely. Nevertheless, scripture has been written and translated largely by heterosexuals with an unexamined traditional assumption that homosexuality is obviously and patently wrong.

Reason and experience have taught us otherwise. Reason, based on scientific research, has taught us that sexual orientation and identity are not chosen; they are biologically imprinted. That is a game changer. It means that homosexuals cannot become straight by exercising faith, although bisexual people may have a choice about which gender they will pursue since they are attracted to both. This new knowledge refutes traditional assumptions about the connection between righteousness and sexual orientation. It means that categorizing LGBTQI identity as sinful is the same as saying these people are rejected by God and the Church from birth, with no possibility of redemption short of a life of celibacy. Many conservatives will immediately recognize this notion as cruel and unusual since it requires people to be celibate their entire lives because they weren't born heterosexual. The theologian John

Wesley gave us a key to this centuries ago when he said that scriptures which are unjust or unloving must be interpreted in light of those which are. In this case, the Golden Rule takes precedence over Leviticus.

Experience has also taught us that the Church has been wrong about LGBTQI people. For centuries, Romans 1 was misinterpreted to mean that homosexuals had denied God and therefore had been given over to shameful lusts and a reprobate mind. We now know that Paul was addressing goddess cult worship involving prostitution, pederasty, and multiple criminal offenses. And now that LGBTQI people are less afraid to admit their identity, we have learned that these are some of the people we love and admire most. Many LGBTQI people love God with a pure and vibrant faith. They are our friends and family. They are not reprobate as a class any more than heterosexual people are. Rather, we now see that they are accepted and approved by God through the seal of the Holy Spirit.

The reason the early Church accepted Gentiles as fully Christian was that God had demonstrated his love and acceptance of them by giving them the Holy Spirit, without their having to reject their Gentile birth and identity. That is, they did not have to become converts to Judaism, and be

circumcised, in order to become Christians. In
Acts 10, we see that God told Peter not to view
something as unclean which God had made clean.
Peter and the others then realized that God had
given the Holy Spirit to the Gentiles, so they were
baptized and fully accepted into the community of
faith. Our experience has taught us the same about
our LGBTQI brothers and sisters. Many who have
accepted and embraced their LGBTQI identity love
the Lord and are filled with the Holy Spirit. They
feel no need to repent of their God-given sexual
identity and orientation. They live vibrant and
exemplary Christian lives as LGBTQI persons in
committed and loving sexual relationships, just
like heterosexuals. If God, knowing that they
cannot meaningfully repent of their orientation or
identity, has accepted these persons by giving
them the Holy Spirit, how can we reject them?
There have always been LGBTQI Christians among
us, but we did not realize it in the same way that
we currently do, because they felt obliged to hide
their orientation and identity. God's acceptance of
LGBTQI persons through the gift of the Holy Spirit
is not new, but our realization of God's acceptance
is.

Let's Close With A Few Questions People Ask:

1. "Won't we be in danger of God's judgment if we agree that homosexuality is not a sin?"

This is an important concern of conservatives. The answer to this question is love. God is love. The Great Commandment is love. The New Commandment is love. The Golden Rule is love. Holy love is the highest Christian ethic and value. It supersedes all else. Back when we used to believe that homosexuality was a result of sin, it seemed loving to warn people to repent and become heterosexual. Now that we know that sexual orientation and identity is a gift of biology and not virtue, we realize that it is hateful and cruel to reject in God's name people whom God has created LGBTQI. Instead, we should introduce people to Jesus Christ regardless of sexual orientation, accept them fully into the life of the Church, and teach them the sexual ethics of celibacy in singleness, and faithfulness in marriage. I hope we are more successful in teaching this to LGBTQI persons than we have been with heterosexuals.

Scripture frequently and consistently portrays God's judgment falling upon those who abuse the weak, the marginalized, the poor and the downtrodden. Concerning the Church's treatment of LGBTQI persons, conservatives used to have ignorance as a defense against God's judgment.

But we are no longer ignorant of the ways scripture has been misinterpreted or of the role that genetics and epigenetics play in sexual orientation and identity. We are no longer ignorant that the Church's treatment of LGBTQI persons leads to their abuse in the larger society as well as to greatly elevated instances of depression and suicide. We are no longer ignorant that God gives the Holy Spirit as readily to LGBTQI persons as to heterosexuals. If we continue to treat LGBTQI persons as unrepentant sinners we, and not they, may come under God's judgment.

God has given the Church the power of binding and loosing because God wants us to use it. We should use the Church's power to bless homosexual persons. It is death-dealing to be the misunderstood, maligned and feared minority at 2.5-5% of the population. I say "feared" because many heterosexuals are afraid that if they associate with homosexuals it will call their own sexual identity into question. Of all the places on earth, the Church should be the preeminent place where LGBTQI people are fully accepted and affirmed as children of God. Instead, they are ostracized at church yet accepted into the family at Google and other progressive corporations. It is shameful that "the world" is more compassionate, more loving and more Christlike on this question than the Church. It is too late for us to lead the vanguard of love for our LGBTQI neighbors. We must humbly admit we were wrong, and sheepishly join the "less righteous" who courageously led the way.

2. "Okay, I understand that LGBTQI people were 'born that way.' I am a straight man, but I was also born in sin. I was born with the sexual desire to have sex with as many women as possible, but God expects me to overcome my natural desires and live a life of righteous obedience. Why can't we expect the same of LGBTQI people?"

We do expect the same of LGBTQI people. You were born with a natural desire to have sex with as many women as possible. A gay man was born with a natural desire to have sex with as many men as possible. The Church should expect both heterosexuals and LGBTQI people to live according to the standard of celibacy in singleness and faithfulness in marriage.

Rather than marry, some conservatives would prefer for LGBTQI people to just live together and take their chances on getting forgiveness from God. I do not see how this is "more virtuous." Bringing more people into committed, loving and stable relationships with one another and with

God seems like a better solution to many conservatives and to most progressives.

3. "Won't homosexual marriage weaken the institution of marriage?"

No. Homosexual marriage will strengthen the institution of marriage. Ideally, marriage creates a stable and committed family unit. This is why marriage is of interest and concern not only to the Church but also to the state. By extending marriage to homosexuals, we would increase the number of people in stable and committed family relationships. This would actually strengthen the fabric of society by reducing the number of people living in casual sexual relationships. It would also strengthen heterosexual marriages, because fewer LGBTQI people would be pretending to be appropriate partners for heterosexual marriage.

Greg notes that, in addition, homosexual marriage is better for children raised in homosexual households. Same sex families raising children have been a fact for a long time. These families may have children from previous failed heterosexual marriages, through surrogate parenthood with one member of the couple having a biological relationship to the child, or through adoption. Children in such families do better than they do in single parent families. Since same-sex marriage has been the law of the land for such a short period of time, we do not yet have solid data regarding the relative status of children of same-sex, married couples, versus the prior situation of children of same-sex, but unmarried couples.

 Logic tells us that the legalization of same-sex marriage, coupled with all of the positive reinforcements that society gives to the institution of marriage, will result in even better outcomes for the children.

4. "Won't acceptance of homosexuality take us back to Roman times?"

No. It will reduce this risk. In Roman times, sexual relationships were governed by power, not virtue. That is why sexual excess was common. Currently, the LGBTQI community does not have the intentional support and influence of the Church in forming monogamous relationships. Instead of bringing moral discipline to LGBTQI relationships, the Church has essentially abandoned this field altogether. By insisting that homosexuality is a sinful choice, the Church essentially abandons the discipling of LGBTQI people and actually creates a larger sub-culture of immorality. If the Church could teach celibacy in singleness and faithfulness in marriage to more LGBTQI people, it would reduce the number of casual sexual encounters rather than increase them. However, we cannot teach Christian values to people whom we are currently rejecting as suitable candidates for discipleship.

5. "Whatever happened to the old idea, 'love the sinner, hate the sin'?"

Loving, conservative Christians have been trying this approach for many years, but it is inadequate because the "sin" in question is one's basic identity as a person. So when we apply this logic to LGBTQI people we are unintentionally saying, "I love you but I hate who you are, right down to the marrow of your bones." This is because sexual orientation and identity are not a choice, but who a person is at their core. LGBTQI people have correctly perceived that we will only love them if they can become straight or celibate, and most of them have realized that this is not a choice they can exercise, much as some might like to. And even if they are not in an active sexual relationship, LGBTQI people are often just plain different from heterosexual people. Conservatives by and large want LGBTQI people to seem straight; some do, many don't. The genuine social and religious acceptance of LGBTQI people isn't just about their not being in an active sexual relationship. It is about the problem of their difference from the other 95% of the population. LGBTQI people have correctly perceived that when we say we hate their LGBTQI orientation and identity, we actually hate them. *They* get it.

Conservatives who ask this question view LGBTQI orientation and identity as a sin which can be repented from, and which can then be removed by God's grace and replaced with a new, heterosexual orientation and identity. Although tradition tells us this is possible, scientific research and experience have demonstrated otherwise. Bisexuals may have a degree of choice because they are attracted to both sexes, and they may account for the conversions we sometimes hear of. That is part of what defines them as bisexual. Hating their sexual orientation and identity, from which they cannot repent, is the same as hating them.

Finally, conservatives are presumptuous concerning what they term "love." Some conservatives treat LGBTQI people horribly and call them terrible things. These conservatives call it "tough love" and claim that if they were LGBTQI, they would want someone to give them the same kind of tough love. But usually, adults can tell us appropriate ways they wish to be treated, and they are the best judges of what loving behavior is for themselves. This kind of "tough love" is nothing less than abuse.

6. "Shouldn't we just say that homosexuality is a sin that God forgives?"

Many loving conservatives feel much more comfortable saying that homosexuality is a sin God forgives. This has two apparent benefits. It keeps the scriptural and traditional understanding of homosexual practice as a sin, but it seems to let the sinner off the hook with the offer of forgiveness. It is a way to have our cake and eat it, too. But there are several reasons this will not work. The first is that this is not an honest interpretation of scripture.

I Corinthians 6:9-10 is traditionally, if incorrectly, understood to say that sodomites will not enter the kingdom of heaven (the passage actually refers to pederasty and temple prostitution, not homosexuality). But if conservatives are going to stick with the traditional, and incorrect, view of this passage we cannot say that homosexual practice can be both continued and forgiven. It is either repented and eschewed or it is not forgiven and these men do not enter the kingdom of heaven. We cannot have it both ways.

Second, this is not honest theologically. If practicing a homosexual orientation and identity were sinful, then this would be an extremely serious kind of sin. It is one thing to be taken unawares by some temptation or other, fall, and subsequently to repent. It is even theologically workable to be taken unawares and fall on several occasions. It is quite another thing to live one's entire adult life in an unrepentant state of habitual sin. A person who lives continually in a state of known sin is a person whose soul is very much in danger. If being a homosexual in a committed relationship were sinful, then this would be an extremely grave state because the sin would be continuous and unrepentant. How can we ethically suggest to people that it is acceptable to live in a continuous state of known sin, and that God will forgive them? The theological solution to this dilemma is to realize that being LGBTQI in a committed relationship is not a sin, but a blessing.

Third, this is inhumane. To say that practicing LGBTQI people are sinning but can be forgiven would mean an LGBTQI person's very nature, which cannot be corrected, is irretrievably sinful. That is, they cannot be made whole. A thief can stop stealing, and an adulterer can stop sleeping with others, but an LGBTQI person cannot stop being an LGBTQI person. If you were to say, "we aren't asking them to stop being LGBTQI, we are just asking them to stop practicing," then that is also unworkable for many people. It is an inhumane burden to tell someone, "Since you are LGBTQI you cannot marry, build a family, or have a loving and committed sexual relationship." This is inhumane. It is time to stop treating LGBTQI people inhumanely. People who don't go to church have figured this out. What is wrong with us?

In closing, I hope that as we look at this conundrum candidly, we can see that these questions take us very far from the spirit of Jesus. Jesus placed love above every other ethic or command, and so do his followers. Knowing as we now do that LGBTQI orientation is no more a choice than the color of our skin, the only possible avenue of love is to realize and admit that being LGBTQI is not a sin. Mistreating these people is.

Printed in Australia
AUHW010104110320
324864AU00061B/513